THE TRANSPACIFIC FLOW

CREATIVE WRITING PROGRAMS IN CHINA

THE TRANSPACIFIC FLOW

CREATIVE WRITING PROGRAMS IN CHINA

Jin Feng

Published by the Association for Asian Studies
Asia Shorts, Number 19
www.asianstudies.org

The Association for Asian Studies (AAS)

Formed in 1941, the Association for Asian Studies (AAS)—the largest society of its kind, with over 6,000 members worldwide—is a scholarly, non-political, non-profit professional association open to all persons interested in Asia.

For further information, please visit www.asianstudies.org.

Cover image courtesy of Xiaolu Ren.

Cataloging-in-Publication Data available from the Library of Congress.

ASIA
SHORTS

Series Editor: David Kenley
Dakota State University

ASIA SHORTS offers concise, engagingly written titles by highly qualified authors on topics of significance in Asian Studies. Topics are intended to be substantive, generate discussion and debate within the field, and attract interest beyond it.

The Asia Shorts series complements and leverages the success of the pedagogically-oriented AAS book series, Key Issues in Asian Studies, and is designed to engage broad audiences with up-to-date scholarship on important topics in Asian Studies. Rigorously peer-reviewed, Asia Shorts books provide cutting-edge scholarship and provocative analyses. They are jargon free, accessible, and speak to contemporary issues or larger themes. In so doing, Asia Shorts volumes make an impact on students, fellow scholars, and informed readers beyond academia.

For further information, visit the AAS website: www.asianstudies.org.

AAS books are distributed by Columbia University Press.

For orders or purchasing inquiries, please visit

https://cup.columbia.edu

COLUMBIA
UNIVERSITY
PRESS

To the Creative Writing Faculty, Staff,
and Students in China, Past,
Present, and Future

About the Author

JIN FENG 冯进 is Professor of Chinese and the
Orville and Mary Patterson Routt Professor of
Literature at Grinnell College, USA. She has published four English monographs: *The New Woman
in Early Twentieth-Century Chinese Fiction* (Pur-
due, 2004), *The Making of a Family Saga* (SUNY,
2009), *Romancing the Internet* (Brill, 2013), and
Tasting Paradise on Earth (U of Washington, 2019),
three Chinese books such as *A Book for Foodies*
吃货之书 (2020), and numerous articles in both
English and Chinese. She is currently researching

and writing on Grinnell College's Chinese connections from the nineteenth to the
twenty-first century.

CONTENTS

Acknowledgments / xiii

List of Abbreviations / xv

1: Introduction: American as Apple Pie? / 1
    The Genesis / 2
    Creative Writing with Chinese Characteristics / 5
    Stepping into the World / 12
    Organization / 21

2: The Model / 23
    "Our Own Tower of Babel" / 25
    "The American Character" / 31
    "Lost in Translation" / 36
    The Mentor and the Recalcitrant Pupil / 40
    Found in Translation / 44

3: The Uneasy Writer / 49
    Elite and Popular Literature in Modern China / 52
    Theories and Debates / 56
    "The Last Avant-Garde" / 60
    An Ode to the Ordinary / 67
    Conclusion / 72

4: The (Not-So-) Reluctant Teacher / 75
    To Teach or Not to Teach / 76
    The Shanghai Experience: Wang Anyi at Fudan / 81
    Writer-Instructors in Hong Kong and Taiwan / 86
    Professional Development for Writer-Instructors / 94

5: Epilogue: We Will Not Be Replaced by ChatGPT? / 99

Notes / 105

Appendix: Catalog of Interviews / 113

Bibliography / 115

Acknowledgments

This book would not have come into being without the generous help from both sides of the Pacific Ocean. I relied on the prompt feedback from Carolyn FitzGerald, Associate Professor of Chinese at Auburn University, who went through multiple versions of several chapters with unerring judgement and seemingly inexhaustible patience. I benefitted from colleagues' input at academic conferences from 2017 onward. I thank the anonymous reviewers for their comments on my book manuscript. I appreciate the support from David Kenley, Editor for the Asia Shorts Series, and from Jonathan Wilson, Publications Manager for the Association for Asian Studies. They provided an intellectual home for my book and guided it across the finish line.

The International Writing Program at the University of Iowa granted me access to their special collections and staff members in 2016–17. Grinnell College awarded me not one, but two year-long sabbatical leaves for the 2019–20 and 2023–24 academic years, which made it possible for me to draft, revise, and prepare the book manuscript for publication. My writing process was also bookended by two residential fellowships in China, one offered by the Chinese Language and Literature Department at Fudan University, my alma mater, in fall 2019, and the other by the Institute for Advanced Studies in Humanities and Social Sciences at Nanjing University in fall 2023. The former kickstarted my book, and the latter allowed me to put on the finishing touches.

Finally, I will remain grateful forever to the Chinese writers and faculty, staff, students, and alumni of university-based creative writing programs in mainland China, Hong Kong, and Taiwan. You granted in-person and virtual interviews despite the COVID-19 pandemic and provided so many other kinds of assistance and encouragement along the way. Your names are too numerous to spell out in entirety. But do know that without you, my book dream would not have seen the light of the day.

List of Abbreviations

BNU: Beijing Normal University, Beijing, China

ECNU: East China Normal University, Shanghai, China

Fudan: Fudan University, Shanghai, China

GC: Grinnell College, Grinnell, Iowa, USA

HKBU: Hong Kong Baptist University, Hong Kong

HKUST: The Hong Kong University of Science and Technology

IWP: The International Writing Program, Iowa City, Iowa, USA

IWPR: International Writing Program Records, Special Collections, the University of Iowa Libraries

IWW: The Iowa Writers' Workshop, Iowa City, Iowa, USA

NKNU: National Kaohsiung Normal University, Kaohsiung, Taiwan

NJU: Nanjing University, Nanjing, China

NTHU: National Tsing Hua University, Hsin-chu, Taiwan

PKU: Peking University [Beijing University], Beijing, China

RUC: Renmin University of China, Beijing, China

SHU: Shanghai University, Shanghai, China

SJTU: Shanghai Jiaotong University, Shanghai, China

Tongji: Tongji University, Shanghai, China

Tsinghua: Tsinghua University, Beijing, China

UI: The University of Iowa, Iowa City, Iowa, USA

UIBE: The University of International Business and Economics, Beijing, China

1

Introduction

American as Apple Pie?

November 30, 2019, Fudan 复旦 University, Shanghai, China. Shao Yanjun 邵燕君, associate professor of modern Chinese literature at the prestigious Peking University (PKU), leaned over to whisper to me: "That was such incredible bad luck the other day." She was referencing my visit to her university a month earlier to interview her former mentor and current colleague, Professor Cao Wenxuan 曹文轩 of the Department of Chinese Literature, an award-winning author of children's literature of international renown and the founder and director of PKU's MFA in creative writing program. It so happened that on the day of my visit, they had received an edict from the university administration that their program was on the chopping block; instead of enrolling another year of students for the MFA in creative writing, PKU had decided that their program would be discontinued to free up space to admit graduate students in other fields. More ironically still, Shao remarked on the "misfortune" their writing program suffered when we were both attending the tenth-anniversary celebration of Fudan's MFA in creative writing, the first of its kind in China. As famous speaker after famous speaker went to the podium to extol the achievements of Fudan's writing program over the past decade, my mind was racing with a whirlwind of thoughts. This current book came into being following this event and many other encounters I had in China over the last six years. But the fascinating story of university-based Chinese creative writing programs starts in the United States.

The Genesis

"I am sick of teaching. I am sick of teaching. I am sick of teaching," bemoaned Vladimir Nabokov to his friend, the literary critic Edmund Wilson.[1] Although he was teaching Russian literature at Cornell University in the 1950s, Nabokov yearned to focus on writing *Lolita*, a novel that would earn him monetary rewards, fame (or notoriety), and the freedom from ever having to teach a college course again. Yet it is precisely the systematic coupling of the profession of authorship with institutions of higher education that makes creative writing programs "as American as baseball, apple pie, and homicide," according to Mark McGurl.[2] This uneasy alliance reveals a tension between the desire to engage in creative endeavors and the systematization of literary study both in the United States and in China, where founders of writing programs have purportedly emulated US models to teach creative writing in Chinese academic institutions.

From the beginning, the American-style writing program was "a national institution with international aspirations and attitudes,"[3] and it was formed under the tremendous urgency of the postwar imperatives for the humanities. During and after the Second World War, a group of influential US intellectuals asserted that creative writing, as no other medium could, enshrined human values that were crucial to civilization. The Iowa Writers' Workshop (IWW), which was founded at the University of Iowa (UI) in 1936 and which established the basic protocols of writing pedagogy, had been conceived as an ideological bulwark against the specter of the Soviet Union. In the words of its longtime director, the American poet and "creative writing Cold Warrior" Paul Engle,[4] to practicing writers, Iowa City felt like "Paris for Hemingway in the 1920s," not least because the IWW taught empathy and spread the gospel of democracy across the globe.[5] Since then, the programmatic mechanisms modeled by this revered writing program have proliferated not only in the United States but also all over the world. Ranging from English-speaking Canada, Australia, New Zealand, and the United Kingdom to countries as diverse as Israel, Mexico, South Korea, and the Philippines, many nations have by now established their own MFA programs in creative writing, emulating the IWW.

In 2009, China launched its first MFA in creative writing at Fudan University. It then saw the entry of professional writers into the faculties of multiplying Chinese writing programs over the next decade and a half. Founders of Chinese writing programs unanimously credit the models of both the IWW and the International Writing Program (IWP), which was cofounded by Engle and his wife, the Sinophone novelist Hua-ling Nieh, at UI in 1967. The IWP invited a total of fifty-seven writers from mainland China between 1979 and 2019, adding to the sixty-four from Taiwan and the twenty-nine from Hong Kong, since its establishment. Some of the IWP's Chinese alumni spearheaded writing programs at Chinese universities, inspired by the US models to establish their own workshop-based teaching. Wang Anyi 王安忆, a 1983 IWP alumna and one of the most influential contemporary Chinese writers, cofounded the MFA in creative writing at Fudan. Several former visiting Chinese scholars to the IWP helped build the Center for Creative Writing at Beijing Normal University (BNU); Mo Yan 莫言, Nobel laureate in literature in 2012 and a 2004 IWP alumnus, has become its director.

What does it mean to import a particular US model of cultural production to China, the purported chief economic and ideological rival of the United States in the twenty-first century? Can the broader political project embraced by such writing programs be divorced from their day-to-day pedagogy? Can this transpacific cultural flow map out a new path for Chinese intellectuals as they navigate the turbulent waters of postsocialist China? And will the flourishing of Chinese writing programs herald a comparable moment of cultural transformation for both China and the world, similar to the way that the inauguration of American creative writing programs signaled a postwar transfer of politico-cultural power from Europe to the United States?

I have investigated these and other crucial questions to produce the first book-length account of the development of Chinese creative writing programs, which has been characterized by the formalization of creative writing instruction and the entrance of professional writers as instructors into universities. Chinese universities had no established creative writing curriculum between 1949 and 2009, except for some short-term training programs for published authors. College-level writing courses aiming to produce good academic writers were typically viewed by the students as necessary evils to fulfill graduation requirements. They had been taught by equally unenthusiastic faculty members who had not published creative work and who were usually marginalized within a Chinese literature department that only rewarded scholarship on literary history and theory. In contrast, adopting a US model seems not only to have revitalized the teaching of writing and elevated its status in Chinese academia but also to have provided individual faculty members with opportunities to produce exciting new scholarship.

Tracing the complex process of the birth and evolution of Chinese creative writing programs, I draw particular attention to the ways that intellectuals have adapted their experiences with the IWW and the IWP after their initial encounters with the "other." Chinese intellectuals sometimes replicate structural biases inherent in their US model, such as the modernist disdain for storytelling and the privileging of psychological delineations, when judging Chinese literary works, even while pursuing literary innovation and program growth. At other times, however, they have used program building to hone writerly craft and to fortify identities. They have demonstrated individual agency and individualist ambitions despite volatile sociopolitical headwinds, and they have eventually changed American creative writing pedagogy both to satisfy the state imperative of mass-producing competent cultural workers and to advance personal career goals. Furthermore, the writers and intellectuals who have contributed to building creative writing programs in mainland China, Hong Kong, and Taiwan deploy specific local resources to craft their founding narratives, even while facing marginalization within the humanistic fields and voicing existentialist concerns over individual and professional relevance, as do their counterparts in the United States. They each emphasize the "added value" of creative writing to enhance the global influence of Chinese national culture, to build up the innovation industry, or to boost students' mental health and personal growth. Sharing a collectivist and utilitarian-oriented view of the function of creative writing, the writing programs at these three East Asian sites also depend more on government patronage and are subjected to more state control than their US models, though the latter do not exist in an autonomous vacuum and also form complex relationships with state sponsorship.

Although the scholarship on the impact of writers' workshops on Western, particularly English-language, literatures has been growing, the influence of this model on the literatures of non-Western nations has been underexplored. Rather than painting it only as a one-way flow of influence and reception, I excavate the multi-sited and multidimensional engagements, appropriations, and competitions that happen between various individual and institutional actors based in the United States, mainland China, Taiwan, and Hong Kong. Putting Sinophone intellectuals at the center of the development of their writing programs and examining their efforts, I untangle their founding narrative from the official discourse of the pursuit for global prominence endorsed by the Chinese state—which is currently engaged in a new Cold War rhetoric with the United States—while dissecting the aesthetic standards set by Western cultural institutions, such as the Nobel Prize in Literature, that have a hold on their mind. This is vital to our imagining of the future of the humanities when the world is at a crossroads between globalization and the rise of totalitarianism.

My book, above all, produces a bird's-eye view of contemporary Chinese literary production, shining a light on institutions as well as individuals. It illuminates how the rise of creative writing programs explains broader issues of Chinese literary and cultural production in the context of an increasingly authoritarian regime's tightening of ideological control; of the demise of state-sponsored mechanisms for nurturing the writing profession and the literature of "socialist realism"; and of the flourishing of popular web literature in a market-oriented economy. Furthermore, it reveals how Chinese intellectuals negotiate political obligations and economic incentives while also seeking academic freedom and recognition from abroad. Chinese intellectuals' apparent embrace of the American-style writing program and its underpinning aesthetic criteria signals a collective anxiety about the role of literature in society as they wrestle with the threat to their livelihood and the decline of traditional cultural prestige.

My book also scrutinizes the complex dynamics of Sino-West cultural exchanges through the unique example of Chinese intellectuals' interactions with an influential American cultural institution. Answering Taiwan scholar Kuan-hsing Chen's call for "Asia as a method," I seek to break free of the simplistic West-versus-East, developed-versus-backward binary through a deeper consideration of multiple perspectives *within* Asia and of Asia's engagements with the West. I study creative writing within a larger framework that entails multi-sited research, mindful both of the IWW's and the IWP's reach in Taiwan and Hong Kong as well as in mainland China, and of the rich and fluctuating interactions between intellectuals inhabiting these three East Asian sites. By integrating findings from Hong Kong and Taiwan into my investigation of creative writing programs in mainland China, my book reveals how varied cultural and geopolitical priorities can rewrite the story of the global influence of the United States. In so doing, my book also offers scholars of literature an understanding of their own field from a comparative perspective: the roles that people-to-people contact, transnational movement, and Cold War politics have played in the formation of a modern literary canon in light of, and in spite of, Western evaluations of the merits (or lack thereof) of modern Chinese literature.

Creative Writing with Chinese Characteristics

In this book, I focus on seven mainland China-based writing programs, respectively hosted by PKU, BNU, Renmin University (RUC)—all located in Beijing—and Fudan University (Fudan), Shanghai University (SHU), Tongji University (Tongji), and East China Normal University (ECNU)—all located in Shanghai—though I also bring other programs into the discussion as it is appropriate. I have chosen these programs because of their central locations, their high profiles, their abundant resources, and finally, their representativeness of all writing programs in mainland China in terms of design and execution. Simply put, they serve as models, inspirations, and training grounds for staff affiliated with other creative writing programs all over China. Additionally, I examine the teaching of creative writing at Hong Kong Baptist University (HKBU) and the Hong Kong University of Science and Technology (HKUST), both located in Hong Kong. In Taiwan, I look at the writing programs at National Tsing Hua University (NTHU), based in Hsin-chu, and National Kaohsiung Normal University (NKNU) in Kaohsiung. The evolutions of creative writing curricula in Hong Kong and Taiwan can provide comparative insights into the localization and Sinicization of creative writing in mainland China.

For each of the above programs, I look at archival and published textual materials, including curricular plans, program reports, publicity brochures, and relevant creative works by their faculty. Furthermore, I have sat in classes and interviewed faculty, students, and alumni. It is worth noting that all the core faculty members of these writing programs are published writers of fiction, essays, or poetry. They also unanimously pay tribute to the IWW, the IWP, and the writing program at the University of East Anglia (UEA). Called by some "the IWW of UK," UEA has drawn inspiration from the IWW and is in fact directed by Daniel Weissbort, who was trained at the IWW and served as interim director of the IWP when Hua-ling Nieh, who was then the director, went on medical leave in 1987.[6] Moreover, most faculty members of the Chinese creative writing programs have visited or hosted faculty members from counterpart programs in the United States. All have at least heard about US writing programs and learned of their pedagogies and theories through famous contemporary Sinophone writers as conduits, such as Yan Geling 严歌苓, Bai Xianyong 白先勇, and Yu Guangzhong 余光中.

The evolution of teaching creative writing in China—starting from an imported concept, growing with additional course offerings, and culminating in undergraduate and graduate programs—manifests a significant breakthrough in Chinese higher education and testifies to the ingenuity and tenacity of those who have built the writing programs at Chinese universities. Both before and during the establishment of university-based creative writing programs in China, vexing questions have been and will continue to dog faculty, students, and program administrators. Can creative writing be taught at all? How can writers legitimize themselves as bona fide faculty members? And, ultimately, what is the use of writing programs when they promise only uncertain financial returns for graduates faced with stiff competition on the job market and the devaluing of the humanities in China? Given societal skepticism and the general shrinking of the humanities, it would come as a surprise that writing programs have not only multiplied at Chinese universities, but they have also successfully recruited famous authors to join the ranks of their faculties. An overview of the goals, curricular designs, and staffing of Chinese writing programs is necessary for a deeper probing into their writer-instructors' fraught relationships with both their home institutions and with wider Chinese society.

My archival research and interviews in the United States reveal that Chinese visitors' intimate experiences with "English as a singular universal language" at US writing programs shaped their vision of Chinese literature and their identity as Chinese writers, complicating the dynamics among those from the different geopolitical locations of mainland China, Hong Kong, and Taiwan.[7] My fieldwork at the three East Asian sites, in turn, shows how they have utilized these writers' American experiences back home after their critical encounters with the "other."

To be sure, program directors, instructors, and students in mainland China may envision the goals and approaches of teaching creative writing differently among themselves. While some consider creative writing a crucial part of humanistic education, others wield it as a tool to realize nationalist goals of amplifying Chinese influence abroad. While the state pushes for mass-producing cultural workers, students may pursue an MFA in creative writing for job prospects. My investigation of writing programs in Hong Kong and Taiwan further adds geopolitical motivations to the complex web of forces shaping Sinophone writing programs and enhances our understanding of the cultural landscape of contemporary China amid escalating global tensions. However, university-based writing programs in China also demonstrate significant overlaps beyond their purportedly shared American models.

Although hailed variously as "the Fudan Path," "the RUC Path," "the SHU Path" or even "the BNU Path," the Chinese creative writing programs show similarities in their goals and course offerings.[8] In terms of curriculum, Chinese writing programs—called *chuangyi xiezuo* 创意写作, *chuangzao xing xiezuo* 创造性写作, or *wenxue chuangzuo* 文学创作 in Chinese, depending on their differing emphases on serious literature or creative industries—may offer BA, MA, MFA, or PhD degrees. Some (RUC and Zhongshan 中山 University in Guangzhou) have branched out to offer courses in creative writing in English, while others (Tsinghua 清华 University in Beijing) have offered courses in "academic writing" to train students in technical writing. Most programs revolve around the "writers' workshop" and high-residency model, though some programs, such as Tongji, utilize a low-residency model; their students meet only on weekends.

Chinese writing programs all claim that they aim to produce "high-caliber talents" (*gao cengci rencai* 高层次人才) who possess professional (*zhuanye hua* 专业化) writing skills in various genres and media, including but not limited to fiction, poetry, the essay, creative nonfiction, print media, broadcast media such as radio and television, film, and new media such as WeChat, a popular social media platform in China. They also list as their essential raison d'état the need to both "optimize human resources in China's cultural industry" and to rise to the challenges of "cultural globalization."[9] Founders of these programs attempt to correct what they consider to be the lack of systematic training in creative writing available to students enrolled in traditional MA programs in Chinese literature on the one hand. On the other, they also view it as their mission to expand the horizons of many native Chinese writers, who "rely solely on personal experiences and local knowledge" for inspiration. In contrast, they claim that their creative writing programs can train writers to "experience unique Chinese reality from the perspective of world literature" and produce "profound reflections on contemporary Chinese people's lives."[10]

Their curricular plans, submitted to the Chinese Ministry of Education for approval and accreditation, also highlight the unmistakable imperative to produce quality cultural workers who can apply literary and artistic theories and professional training to practical jobs such as writing scripts, reports, and various other documents necessary not just for cultural production but also for bureaucratic management. While touting "politically correct" criteria, such as work ethics, and general requirements like foreign language proficiency and computer skills, which are applicable to all students seeking a master's degree in different disciplines in China, creative writing programs emphasize the tripartite structure underlying their course offerings: a systematic knowledge of intellectual and literary histories, high-level writing skills, and a certain degree of artistic literacy.[11] They claim that this kind of curricular design will train their graduates to work effectively in a variety of professions as writers, editors, newscasters, game designers, administrative assistants, managers, and civil servants.

To realize their educational goals, the writing programs at Chinese universities have combined the studio- and academic-style programs of creative writing commonly seen in the United States.[12] Studio programs mimic conservatories and focus exclusively on the writing craft, while academic programs require other coursework as well. The typical curriculum of a Chinese writing program includes coursework, an internship, and a creative thesis. Mandatory courses can be divided into those that satisfy general education requirements in foreign languages (usually English) and "political thought" (such as Marxist art theory), which are mandated by the Chinese Ministry of Education, and major requirements that include theory, practice, and a combination of both, such as Contemporary Fiction Study and Practice. Students can also take elective courses offered by MFA in creative writing programs, by MA in Chinese literature programs, or by other programs and departments at the university. All in all, the coursework includes theory classes, including art theory and art appreciation; literary histories and literary studies of both Chinese literature and foreign literature in translation; "practicum" courses that afford students the opportunity to improve their craft by trying their hand at writing fiction, poetry, creative nonfiction, drama, or web literature, and sometimes through translation practices; and the opportunity to interact with established contemporary authors, artists, and editors, who come as guest speakers to a summit forum organized by the writing programs. Each program also boasts several internship sites at literary journals and at the local branch of the Chinese Writers' Association. Finally, these programs typically require a creative thesis for graduation, which consists of a substantial body of creative work (a novel or a volume of collected fiction or poetry)—whether published in print or not—and a reflection article on the process and theory of creative writing.

Why have writing programs at Chinese universities become so popular? This has happened thanks to a confluence of factors, including state policies, local initiatives, and a felicitous coupling of established professional writers and institutions of higher education. First, the Chinese Ministry of Education attempts to have more students graduate with professional degrees, ready to work as cultural workers rather than just doing research in academia.[13] Second, enrolling students in MFA degree programs would yield positive results for students seeking employment after graduation and hence enhance the reputation of the participating faculty, programs, and schools. Furthermore, the new concept of creative writing can help revamp the tired mandatory course of College Composition (Daxue Xiezuo 大学写作) and allow scholars and faculty members to have something new to research and play with.[14] Last but not least, a mutually agreeable arrangement between professional writers and institutions of higher education has been established.

The practice of having writers teach writing to degree-seeking students, though prevalent in writing programs at Chinese universities nowadays, is a fairly recent phenomenon in China. Between 1949 and 2009, there had not existed any comprehensive creative writing curriculum, let alone any degree-granting programs, at Chinese universities. Creative writing courses were occasionally offered at the college level, such as at BNU in the 1980s, but they remained sporadic and localized.[15] The Lu Xun 鲁迅 Academy of Literature run by the state-sponsored Chinese Writers' Association—though commonly regarded as the mecca for aspiring writers for a long time—has a high threshold for entrance, admitting just those with the right political background and publishing record, and it only offers short-term training of up to one year. In fact, Chinese universities, and especially their Chinese literature departments, had typically claimed that it was not their mission to train creative writers since the early 1950s, when Chinese higher education underwent massive restructuring. The adjustment of colleges and departments (yuanxi tiaozheng 院系调整) in the 1950s followed the USSR's educational model to reorganize Chinese higher education and speed up industrialization in China. It decreased the number of comprehensive universities while increasing the number of schools that could train technical specialists. The number of comprehensive universities dropped from forty-nine in 1949 to fourteen in 1953, while colleges of technology, agriculture, and teacher training increased by 35.7 percent, 61.1 percent, and 175 percent, respectively.[16] Unsurprisingly, liberal arts institutions were eliminated, while education in the humanities in general suffered a great loss.

In contrast, from 2009 to 2016, within only a seven-year span after Fudan's MFA in creative writing was launched, more than one hundred universities started to offer creative writing courses, there were at least thirty established creative writing programs, and there were close to two hundred institutions actively seeking to establish communities in the creative writing field.[17] Today, dozens of Chinese universities have established undergraduate and graduate programs in creative writing. Research output on creative writing has increased by leaps and bounds. Community-based learning, such as university outreach efforts into K–12 schools and overseas communities, has also led to the bourgeoning of related organizations and international conferences, culminating in the establishment of the annual World Sinophone Writing Conference (Shijie Huawen Xiezuo Dahui 世界华文写作大会). Furthermore, all Chinese writing programs have recruited established writers to teach courses or serve as thesis advisors. Other than Wang Anyi at Fudan and Mo Yan and Yu Hua 余华 at BNU, RUC has hired Yan Lianke 阎连科, ECNU has hired Sun Ganlu 孙甘露, and so forth. The program directors are usually also published authors themselves, such as Wang Hongtu 王宏图 of Fudan, Cao Wenxuan of PKU, and Zhang Qinghua 张清华 of BNU.

The Chinese creative writing programs solicit the help of famous contemporary writers to serve several ends. For one, they can head off skepticism about faculty members' qualifications and credentials. As is often the case, outsiders believe the old adage: "those who cannot do, teach." Second, they hope to bask in the reflected cultural prestige of the famous authors and thus maximize the "halo effect" of their programs. Moreover, by appointing two thesis advisors for each student— one a faculty member from the university and the other an established writer—the writing programs can generate additional social capital, establish more internship bases, and tap into wider networks brought in by the writer. Consequently, this arrangement makes the programs more attractive to potential applicants, and their students more marketable after graduation. For the writers involved in this arrangement, the chance to benefit from the fame of top universities while enjoying stable employment and cultural prestige—not to mention deeper friendship and engagement with university-employed literary scholars who critique and study their works—would never be unwelcome in the increasingly commercialized and competitive cultural market in China.[18]

The ostensibly win-win arrangement between writers and universities realized in and through Chinese writing programs has not come easily or "naturally" by any means, however. Not only must founders jump through a series of hoops to get started, but there also is no guarantee of continued support from the institution once the program is launched. The founding of Fudan's MFA program in creative writing came to pass only after several rounds of back-and-forth with accreditation agents at the Chinese Ministry of Education. Due to turf wars between scholars of literature and those of the fine arts, Fudan's MFA in creative writing is affiliated with theatre (Xiju 戏剧) in fine arts, since creative writing is seen as drastically different from painting, dance, or music. Likewise, Tongji's creative writing program is branded as an MFA in "artistic design," again testifying to the awkward position creative writing programs occupy in Chinese universities, even as they are allowed bigger quotas to enroll students seeking professional rather than academic degrees. PKU's MFA in creative writing program, started in 2014, was classified as "Writing for TV and Film," and graduates received diplomas from the School of Journalism and Communications or a degree in fine arts. The program's most recent skirmish with university administrators even more starkly illustrates the precariousness of writing programs' survival at institutions of higher education in China. As late as 2023, ECNU has finally become the first institution to establish a stand-alone master's in creative writing in their Department of Chinese Literature; it is not affiliated with theatre, broadcast media, or design, and it is equal to, rather than subordinate to, the program in modern and contemporary Chinese literature within the department. This newest development has inspired other university-based Chinese writing programs to pursue a similar path forward. To their gratification, the Chinese Ministry of Education has finally approved this change in designation in the newest version of their "Graduate Programs and Requirements," released in January 2024, if only still on a "trial" (*shiyong* 试用) basis.[19]

Despite, or perhaps precisely because of, explicit or implicit risks, administrators and faculty members of Chinese writing programs fight to survive and thrive. Their new dilemma did not stop PKU faculty members from trying to conceive of a new Institute for the Teaching and Learning of Literature (Wenxue Jiangxi Suo 文学讲习所) to continue their writing program in some fashion. Nor did it prevent its former director, Cao Wenxuan, from touting their successful graduates, such as Xu Zechen 徐则臣, who won a Mao Dun 茅盾 Literary Prize in 2019, the most prestigious award for novels in China, and Wen Zhen 文珍, who is now working as an editor at the famed Chinese journal *Renmin Wenxue* 人民文学 (People's Literature). BNU, in comparison, has taken a slightly different approach to safeguard their prospects. They insist on enrolling MA rather than MFA students, and they market the program as specializing in "literary writing" rather than in "creative writing," dismissing the latter as merely catering to lowbrow commercial interests, even though they sent a PhD student, Chu Yunxia 褚云侠, to study the teaching of creative writing for a whole year in Iowa City. BNU's three-year writing program admits eight to ten students each year, with lower entrance exam scores (five to ten points lower) than the regular cutoff grade for MA program candidates nationally. Their curriculum, however, does not differ so widely from those offered by the MFA in creative writing programs at other schools. Zhang Qinghua, the executive director of their Creative Writing Center (Mo Yan has been the nominal director since receiving the Nobel Prize in Literature), claims that one-third of their graduates become full-time writers, one-third work for the Chinese Writers' Association or become civil servants, and one-third pursue PhD degrees.

However, he does not hesitate to promote their success in producing some of the rising stars in contemporary Chinese literature as both authors and scholars: Cui Jun 崔君 and Chen Shuai 陈帅 have become professional writers, and Wan Fang 万芳 is pursuing a PhD in Britain. Moreover, they have continued to work with the Lu Xun Academy of Literature to train professional writers. In the past, the joint program between the two only admitted established and experienced writers who wished to take a "refresher" to polish up their writing skills and theoretical training, boasting among their alumni famous writers such as Mo Yan, Yu Hua, Liu Zhenyun 刘震云, and Chi Zijian 迟子建. Since 2016, their MA in literary writing has incorporated teaching staff and resources from the Lu Xun Academy and has been able to provide students with more opportunities to network with successful writers, editors, and publishers, and thus to pave the way for students' gainful employment after graduation.

Stepping into the World

Administrators and faculty members at Chinese creative writing programs may appear more collectivist when compared to their US counterparts. For instance, in mission statements, they typically emphasize the program's contributions to state initiatives—without a doubt to fight for survival under the government's tight control of the dissemination of ideas—instead of advocating for nourishing creativity, authenticity, and individual fulfillment. But the overlaps between the revered American models and their adaptations in the Chinese context can manifest themselves in surprising, as well as in expected, places. To launch and build up a successful academic program, both the American and Chinese founders must invoke national cultural imperatives and appeal to institutional priorities, even as they proclaim distinct pedagogical goals and emphasize different aspects of the curriculum. The early history of the IWW reveals not only the equally precarious position that creative writing programs occupy within US institutions of higher education as Chinese programs in theirs, but it also reveals the similar strategies deployed by the program founders to "sell" their vision to top university administrators, if not to the national government.

As expected, "the workshop style" of teaching creative writing, pioneered by the IWW, has later been propagated by Chinese writer-instructors such as Wang Anyi. John Schultz (1932–2017), a writer of fiction and nonfiction, a former faculty member in the Fiction Writing Department at Columbia College Chicago, and the creator of the Story Workshop method of writing instruction, was introduced to Fudan's Chinese Literature Department by his former student, the Sinophone writer Yan Geling. Schultze taught fiction writing at Fudan for a period in 2008 before the class was taken over by Wang Anyi in 2009. In addition to overlapping pedagogical approaches and staffing connections, Chinese and American writing programs have also shared a strikingly similar trajectory of birth, and they are full of similar tensions. The expansion of US creative writing programs benefited from Cold War initiatives such as the GI Bill and the National Defense Education Act, issued by the US federal government to subsidize the expansion of American universities to compete with the Soviet Union. Moreover, their pedagogy was formulated against the purportedly collectivist and "propagandist" Soviet ideology by emphasizing the individual over the collective and the concrete over the abstract. Half a century later, Chinese writing programs multiplied, thanks to a "rising" China's initiative to mass-produce high-quality cultural workers and hence give the nation a boost in its bid for cultural as well as economic prominence, and its drive to realize its ambitious goal of "Made in China 2025" in both economic and cultural arenas.

On a more micro level, Chinese writing programs and their American models such as the IWW have faced similar trials and tribulations in their respective struggles for survival and success. For one thing, writing faculty, whether they teach at Chinese or American institutions of higher education, must fight for academic and intellectual legitimacy. Although UI listed creative writing courses in their catalog as early as the 1895–1896 academic year—such as the Verse-Making Class first offered by their English Department in the spring of 1897—the writing program itself did not come into official existence until 1941. Wilbur Schramm, the IWW's first director, spent considerable energy defending the program to UI's administration at the time, arguing for "the right status of imagination within the academy and the importance of approaching literature from a humane rather than scientific point of view."[20] He also asserted that having writers teach writing would provide good role models and demonstrate the importance of practicing writing to the students. Although no one can be taught to write—or to practice any profession for that matter—he pointed out, "the teacher directs, aids, encourages; the student learns by his own effort," and the program can "open the riches of the university to the younger writer."[21] Echoing his defense of humanistic approaches in US academia, Norman Foerster, one of the founders of the IWW, was opposed to the "scientific" turn of studying literature in their English Department, which privileged criticism over creative writing at the time. A traditionalist in his defense of a liberal education based on a broad study of the humanities, he believed that "both criticism and creative work should occupy a central position in higher education," and he insisted that creative writing would "assist an inner comprehension of art."[22] Even Paul Engle, the famous poet and cultural entrepreneur known for his knack for recruiting talent, raising funds, and gaining publicity for the IWW, had to physically carry two suitcases of published works into the office of the UI provost Harvey Davis to convince Davis of the impact and value of the creative writing program in enhancing UI's reputation.[23]

It was under Engle's able leadership that the emphasis of the IWW changed from treating creative writing as just another part of a broader scholarly discipline to viewing scholarship as a side benefit to the writer. In fact, the increasing professionalization of creative writing sought to reinforce IWW's time-honored *cri de coeur* that "the creation of literature is as academically respectable and important as the study of literature."[24] Nowadays, we see "a gradual reorientation in U.S. higher education away from the liberal arts and toward practical, pre-professional, and vocational courses of study" because students and their parents often want a good-paying job after graduation, but writing programs have endured at American universities.[25] This is because, according to Dean MacCannell, "their value is a function of the quality and quantity of experience they promise," for we now live in "the world of experience economy," in which programs, trips, courses, and reports all constitute a sort of "generalized tourism" for students.[26] But the continued existence of creative writing in US academia can also be attributed to the kind of "delicate and imaginative aggression" Engel was known for, and which program administrators have learned to deploy, though perhaps not with the same degree of success as Engle.[27]

Similarly, when faculty members first attempted to establish writing programs at Fudan and other top-tier institutions in China, they not only had to contend with the common societal skepticism concerning whether creative writing can be taught and whether writers can be produced in a college classroom but also with the prevailing academic convention that prioritizes research over creative writing within Chinese literature departments. In fact, faculty members and alumni of Fudan's writing program reminisce even today how their first introduction to the department started with authoritative statements from senior faculty and famous scholars, who in no uncertain terms dispelled any illusion that the pedagogical goals—and indeed, the raison d'état of the Chinese Department—lay in teaching writing and producing writers. The unfriendly milieu facing faculty members of writing programs can also be detected in their recruitment and evaluation criteria. Today, Chinese universities typically require a PhD degree as a minimum qualification when hiring faculty members, and they do not accept an MFA in creative writing as a terminal degree that fulfills that requirement. After entering academia, if they are so lucky as to have earned a PhD along the way, instructors of creative writing must also produce research articles and scholarly books in addition to creative works, and the evaluation of their scholarship is weighted more heavily toward the former rather than the latter. Given the heavy teaching load early career faculty members must shoulder, this treatment often creates undue burdens and insurmountable impediments for those teaching writing at Chinese universities while seeking tenure and promotion, despite their reputations as published poets or fiction writers.

Whereas all the Chinese creative writing program have navigated external and intramural politics and have cut through bureaucratic red tape to come to fruition, each reveals unique circumstances surrounding its inception and presents a specific vision for its growth. Significantly, administrators and faculty members frequently self-consciously tie the fate of their programs to the status of Chinese literature in the world and its relationship with world literature, even while they debate the merits of contemporary Chinese literature and the criteria for judging it among themselves. Below, I present revealing vignettes culled from interviews with faculty and program directors of high-profile Chinese creative writing programs that bring these common themes into sharp relief. In some cases, I have withheld the true identities of my interview subjects for reasons of privacy and confidentiality. These excerpts can provide another layer of context for the examination of writer-instructors' efforts throughout the remainder of this book.

At Fudan, Chen Sihe 陈思和, one of the cofounders of the school's writing program, states that he initially started the program to provide a platform for and to fully utilize the talent of Wang Anyi, who enjoys teaching writing at Fudan. She has been offering courses there since 1994 and was officially appointed a professor and advisor to MA students in creative writing in 2004. When a group of faculty members from Fudan's Chinese Department, led by Chen, paid multiple visits to China's Ministry of Education in Beijing to lobby for the establishment of their MFA in creative writing, they heard that their effort fortuitously dovetailed with the national educational initiative of training more professional degree-holders rather than purely academic-research talents. Chen attributes the ultimate success in launching Fudan's MFA program in no small part to that overarching national policy.

Some faculty members in writing at Fudan, such as Zhang Yiwei 张怡微, who is also a well-published "post-80s" (*Baling hou* 八零后) author, argue for the intrinsic value of writing courses as an integral part of humanistic education. Even while acknowledging that Fudan's writing program does not necessarily produce professional writers, she holds that writing programs like theirs can train students in knowledge, logic, and taste in literature. There are practical considerations at play as well. According to Wang Hongtu—a professor of Chinese literature, a published novelist, and the director of Fudan's writing program—the concept of an MFA in creative writing, though it is an "import" (*bolaipin* 舶来品), has helped faculty in the Chinese Literature Department exceed the state quota on enrolled MA students. Yet he also admits that of all their students pursuing an MFA in writing, "one third are truly interested in creative writing; one third feel that other fields are harder to get in than this one, because MFA requires lower entrance scores than MA programs; and one third just want to have a good-looking diploma and stay in Shanghai after graduation."

One can detect the same combination of idealistic aspirations and pragmatic considerations in other writing program directors in Shanghai. For Zhang Sheng 张生, the director of Tongji's MFA in creative writing, their program reconnects with and revives a native tradition of having established authors, including Zhu Ziqing 朱自清, Shen Congwen 沈从文, and Shen Yinmo 沈尹默, teach creative writing as regular full-time faculty members at universities, which started before 1949. This "glorious tradition," in his mind, was unfortunately disrupted by the adjustments of colleges and departments in the 1950s. Although the adjustment made good use of available resources in the short term, and though it corrected to some extent the unbalanced geographical placement of institutions of higher education in China before 1949, in the long run, it restricted the growth of the intellectual lives of both institutions of higher learning and the students they educated. It ignored the unique needs and workings of educational institutions, emphasized uniformity in its ideological bent, compromised academic freedom, and especially harmed humanities fields in terms of resource allocation, staffing, and their sociocultural status in China. But Zhang is no mere defender of the humanities. In attempting to adapt the American model of teaching creative writing, he also hopes to spread Chinese cultural influence abroad and make Chinese literature on a par with Japanese literature by training Chinese writers in a more systematic and less haphazard way.

Ge Hongbing 葛红兵, the founder and driving force behind SHU's far-flung creative writing program, even more frankly expresses considerations for survival and growth when describing his vision. Thanks to his initiative and tireless work, SHU's program is the only one in China that offers BA, MFA, and PhD degrees in creative writing. Moreover, they reach out to K–12 schools and offer courses to train young writers while also seeking to establish connections with Sinophone writers and organizations overseas. He believes that their efforts have followed the national policy to train high-caliber workers for cultural production, and he objects to the traditional divide and hierarchy between highbrow serious literature and lowbrow popular literature. Instead, their program collaborates with Yuewen 阅文 Company, the largest state-sponsored publisher of web literature in China, to offer an MFA that can focus on writing web-based genre fiction as well as on serious literature. He believes that all contemporary authors must depend on the market; so-called "serious literature" and "popular literature" have both evolved over the years, and in any case, "nowadays 80% of writing and 90% of reading happen online." But he also acknowledges that the government's tightening control of the internet and content published in other media since 2017 has posed impediments to creative writing.

In comparison to the relatively liberal and market-oriented leanings of the Shanghai-based programs discussed above, the creative writing programs based at higher education institutions in Beijing seem to cling more closely to traditional boundaries between serious and popular literature. Founders and directors of writing programs in Beijing all describe the goals of their programs as nurturing talented writers of serious literature. Diao Keli 刁克利 of RUC, a specialist in author studies and a translator of a series of textbooks in creative writing published by RUC Press, believes that RUC specializes in training authors of "serious literature," even though he acknowledges that popular literature such as web literature also has a place in creative writing programs "because different programs have different goals and strengths." He proposes to train students at different levels and in different genres. If writing programs can produce good editors or propagandists in addition to those dedicated to the full-time writing of serious literature, that would be all for the better, he adds.

Cao Wenxuan echoes Diao's estimation that contemporary Chinese writers need more rigorous training, as he sees a clear demand to make modern Chinese literature more elegant (*dianya* 典雅) and noble (*gaogui* 高贵), lamenting that Chinese writers "have lived in the wilderness (*manhuang zhidi* 蛮荒之地)" for too long. In his mind, only Chinese academia can provide the necessary education and polish for "free-range" Chinese writers. Moreover, he claims that their program aims to train literary scholars as well as writers. They can turn students from a "reader" (*yuedu zhe* 阅读者) into an "interpreter" (*jiedu zhe* 解读者) of literature by teaching them how to read and appreciate works with the appropriate attitude and method (*zhengdang de zishi* 正当的姿势). Their students later enrolled in PhD programs and became editors or writers, he reveals. Similarly, Zhang Qinghua is eager to differentiate between "literary writing" and "creative writing." He dismisses creative writing as producing mostly genre fiction and popular literature and sees it as their mission to train only writers of "serious literature" that promotes "humanistic values." Yet despite the Beijing academics' general gravitation toward highbrow literature, there has also been clear-sighted recognition of contemporary market situations. Shao Yanjun, for instance, points out the crisis facing state-funded literary journals, a sharp shrinkage of readership in serious literature, and the demise of a traditional, bottom-up way of cultivating authors in contemporary China.

Whatever their specific mission statements or geographical locations, program directors' assessments of their success in realizing their mission also correlates with their evaluation of the quality of contemporary Chinese literature and its relationship to world literature. Fudan evoked the concept of "world literature" when arguing to the Ministry of Education about the necessity of founding the first MFA in creative writing.[28] The awareness of and attention to Chinese literature's global position have been shared widely among faculty members of other Chinese writing programs as well. Generally, the higher esteem the writing faculty members give to contemporary Chinese literature, and the more optimistic they sound about its ranking among world literature, the more confidence they express about the efficacy of their writing programs. On the other end of the spectrum are those holding dismal views of contemporary Chinese literary works while also painting a more realistic picture of their own writing programs. This is perhaps to be expected. After all, Chinese creative writing programs have all vowed to produce quality cultural workers who can help China compete with other nations and become more fully integrated into the global literary and cultural scene.

Some of those interviewed believe that Chinese literature does not deserve being ranked among world literature at all because contemporary works are "too simple," unable to move readers emotionally or stimulate them intellectually. Since these works "lack creativity," they cannot give foreigners what they cannot find in their own national literatures and can only be regarded as "cultural spectacles." The fiction by Mo Yan, Wang Anyi, and Jia Pingwa 贾平凹 is of good quality to be sure, but it is nothing special compared with foreign works recognized as world literature. They even hold that "reading contemporary works will lower your [intellectual or literary] level." Interestingly, these low opinions are typically held by faculty members who have been educated at, or who have at least visited, US institutions of higher education. It appears that those who have been exposed to Western education and literature in systematic or immersive ways also tend to believe that contemporary Chinese authors compare unfavorably to Chinese authors from the 1920s and 1930s in terms of their educational background, cultural knowledge, and global perspective. These "pessimists" also advocate that Chinese authors read Western works widely since "the tradition of fiction came from Europe."

Additionally, they do not agree with the notion that Chinese literature cannot step into the world due to bad translations, deeming it a pretext (*zhexiu bu* 遮羞布) for low-quality works and viewing those who wish to maintain "unique Chinese characteristics" in literary works as "lacking in confidence." In other words, they do not believe contemporary Chinese authors possess the necessary quality to become world-class writers, and they do not think it is the fault of translation that Chinese writers are not widely appreciated abroad: "there are no Chinese or foreign writers, just good and bad writers." They also believe the Nobel Prize in Literature has reasonable and equitable criteria for great literature: profound thinking, great writing skills, and "idealism." Consequently, they prescribe contemporary authors to "raise their own quality" by traveling widely and living in foreign countries to understand "how foreigners think." Not surprisingly, these liberal-minded faculty members also rail against strict state ideological control and blame it for blocking Chinese writers' creativity.

Others have expressed more optimism about Chinese literature. Zhang Yiwei attributes foreign scholars' denigration of contemporary Chinese literature to different tastes and cultural traditions while remarking that foreign interest in premodern works has always been high. Chen Sihe, a literary critic and scholar of contemporary Chinese literature, claims that Chinese literature has always been part of world literature, and "some [of our compatriots] are just being too anxious, vainglorious, and have an inferiority complex" when they belabor the need to have Chinese literature "step into the world." On the role of translation, he states, "Of course, to have foreign readers read Chinese literature you need translation, but it's hard to say whose works they are after being translated. In fact, being translated does not mean it is good work, and even praise from foreigners is no guarantee that it is good work." He likens evaluating Chinese literature to judging Chinese wonton soup: "Foreigners might be good at judging pizzas but not necessarily Chinese wontons." That is, Western aesthetic tastes are not necessarily the best or most reliable criteria for judging Chinese literature. He thinks creative writing and literary works are currently at their peak in China, but the best authors are still those born in the 1950s and 1960s. In contrast, in his eye, younger authors "have issues" in their ways of thinking, perhaps referencing the "inferiority complex" he noted earlier. Equally optimistic, though speaking from a different perspective, Ge Hongbing believes that the gap between Chinese literature and world literature is shrinking. He points out positive trends he sees in the evolution of Chinese literature: Sinophone diasporic literature has integrated into world literature, Chinese web-based genre fiction has become a popular cultural export and a base for enfranchisement, and professional writers have entered Chinese academia, all with state sponsorship. Contemporary Chinese literature, he further notes, may well follow the trajectory of American literature in the wake of the civil rights movement in the United States, as it integrates contemporary political and cultural shifts the same way American literature benefitted from the burgeoning of anti-war literature, feminist literature, and Black literature.

Echoing their votes of confidence in the future of Chinese literature are several academics working at institutions in Beijing. Cao Wenxuan believes that the Chinese state and translators have done a tremendous job of translating and introducing foreign works into China, and that no other nation knows more about world literature "since we have translated the works by almost all the notable figures in other literary traditions." Moreover, he holds that, nowadays, Chinese writers have become more discerning when choosing with whom to publish abroad. They have increasingly published with better publishing houses abroad rather than accepting any bidder on the first try. Therefore, they have successfully "stepped in" (*zou jinqu* 走进去) or been integrated into mainstream cultures abroad and can "step out" (*zou chuqu* 走出去) and spread Chinese cultural influence more effectively.

Cao confidently concludes that Chinese literature is entering world literature. "The best Chinese literature is world-class literature," he states. There is a "difference" (*chabie* 差别) but not a "distance" (*chaju* 差距) between Chinese literature and world literature, and "it is not fair for others to judge Chinese literature by lumping all the best of world literature and stack Chinese literature against that. We should only compare best literary works from any nations." Unfortunately, he further claims, Chinese people lack confidence in their own literature. Critics are often too moderate in their tones—no high praise or sharp criticism, clinging to "the golden mean" (*zhongyong* 中庸). Furthermore, foreigners also have biases against China. Stereotypes about China linger because China had been closed off from the world for too long. The foreign impression of China was that of disasters and suffering: "They cannot embrace Chinese literature without any reservations, unlike the way we do theirs." Ominously, in his eye, China is on the verge of becoming more closed up again, and "the Chinese state does not value or cherish our writers enough."

On the issue of the foreign judgment of Chinese literature, Cao believes that Mo Yan draws a negative picture of China, but then again, all great writers, including Nobel Prize laureates, criticize their own nations and cultures. He cannot say for sure what the criteria for good literature are and can only rely on his "instincts" to make judgments. The Nobel Prize is not perfect, but to him it's the only commonly accepted award worldwide. Furthermore, the committee that decides the Nobel Prize in Literature has come to favor more diverse and "less popular" works, and to promote literature that advances our cognitive understanding of the world rather than merely providing aesthetic pleasures. He states, "We have to accept [Western] criteria in order to spread our cultural influence, because they have the dominant voice (*huayu quan* 话语权). But modern literature is modern not because of new literary devices such as stream of consciousness but because of new themes and new directions with which to explore the human experiences, and this is true of modern Chinese literature as well."

Compared to Cao's philosophical acceptance of foreign biases, Zhang Qinghua sounds more like a staunch supporter of nativist traditions. He believes that starting in the 1980s, Chinese literature has become world-class literature since Chinese writers have come to adopt a global perspective while China reopened to the world. The 1980s witnessed changing trends in Chinese literature, and the 1990s reaped a bumper harvest, but the turn of the twenty-first century brought suspicion and uncertainty as China made a turn toward becoming a more totalitarian state. He asserts that literature is closely tied to history and social experiences. European literature might focus on the richness of private life, but Europeans' world is too stable and eventless. In contrast, China has undergone massive transformations over the last forty years; suffering, losses, and loneliness abounded, but so did great joys and carnivalesque celebrations. China has "distilled hundreds of years of history" into the last forty years, and this "could happen only once in a thousand years." To him, it was no accident that Mo Yan won a Nobel Prize, for he and other serious writers critique Chinese culture just like Lu Xun and the other authors in the May Fourth Movement of early twentieth-century China. He therefore considers Wolfgang Kublin, a harsh critic of contemporary Chinese literature, to be fatally biased since he had only partial knowledge: "He has read Lu Xun, but very little premodern literature and practically no contemporary literature." On translation, Zhang believes that it almost always diminishes the original and only occasionally enhances it. Translation is not the deciding factor when judging literature, though; neither is state support or the lack thereof. However, he still believes that the government must support translation efforts by rewarding good translators.

Ranging from being belligerently confident to cautiously optimistic to dismissive and disparaging when it comes to contemporary Chinese literature—and with some of them holding contradictory views simultaneously or moving back and forth in our interviews—these Chinese writer-administrator-teachers illustrate the complexity of their positions on the relationship between Chinese literature and world literature. However, they have also consistently applied a global perspective to reflect on critical issues such as the role of translation, the criteria for good literature, and China's position in the world, all of which shape the ways they teach creative writing and build up writing programs at Chinese universities.

Organization

Integrating field research as well as historical and literary analyses, my book takes a broad chronological sweep, following Chinese intellectuals' steps from their visits to the IWP and the IWW, their gradual entry into Chinese universities, and their shifting roles in cultural production in twenty-first-century China. Throughout this line of inquiry, I interrogate the ways these writer-teachers negotiate their various identities as they face competing, and at times overwhelming, ideological, cultural, and economic forces.

Chapter 1, "Introduction: American as Apple Pie?" surveys the conception, evolution, curricular design, and administrative mechanisms of university-based creative writing programs in China. It also examines the state and institutional motivations for creating writing programs modeled on US cultural institutions such as the IWP and the IWW.

Chapter 2, "The Model," investigates how Chinese writers' first encounters with US writing programs shaped their views of Chinese literature and translation, and their identities as Chinese nationals and writers. Their reflections reveal an increasing awareness of the outside world along with a rising uneasiness regarding the stature of Chinese literature in the world. Yet they also utilized their residency at the IWP as a staging ground to establish networks and explore literary innovations. Chapter 3, "The Uneasy Writer," delineates how contemporary Chinese authors navigate the volatile ecosystem that sees the decline of state-funded literary journals and serious literature and the rise of popular internet literature and its associated franchises. In theoretical debates, they wrestle not only with Western paradigms of literary studies—such as Roland Barthes's notion of "the death of the author"—and the dominant Western biases that devalue storytelling and political expression but also with Chinese societal skepticism about the value of creative writing programs. Some have also illustrated through their creative output how to adapt to the "new normal." Sun Ganlu and Wang Anyi are established contemporary authors who made a "popular turn" in award-winning novels. Teaching at and directing creative writing programs at prestigious universities in mainland China, they seem to have pivoted from the avant-garde and experimental to the popular and politically correct mainstream in their recent works.

Chapter 4, "The (Not-So-) Reluctant Teacher," in turn draws on extensive fieldwork to scrutinize how Chinese writers make their way into academia amid increasing pressure from the marketplace and tightening ideological control from the party-state. After analyzing their reflections on prior experiences at the IWW and the IWP, it examines the specific ways writers such as Wang Anyi adapt and execute the "workshop" model in the classroom. It also reveals the institutional and individual factors that shape writer-teachers' efforts to build writing programs in mainland China, Taiwan, and Hong Kong. Finally, chapter 5, "Epilogue: We Will Not Be Replaced by ChatGPT?" briefly surveys the postpandemic cultural landscape facing creative writing programs in China. It also looks to the future of creative writing. Is it an intrinsic benefit to be shared as much as possible since it responds to our deepest desire for self-expression and self-understanding? Or is it something more noxious, given the all-powerful state intervention and surveillance in contemporary China?

2

THE MODEL

The American-style writing program embodied by the Iowa Writers' Workshop (IWW) and the International Writing Program (IWP) has provided much-needed fortification for beleaguered Chinese writing instructors. Not only does it present a successful model in creative writing pedagogy and programmatic development, but it also helps its Chinese emulators accrue cultural prestige, thanks to the American model's long and storied tradition and great international influence. The IWP especially shaped Chinese intellectuals' views about their identities as writers and writing instructors and about the relationship between Chinese literature and world literature. In fact, most if not all of them gained their first glimpses of US creative writing programs through the IWP, either through immersive in-person experiences as invited scholars or writers in residence in Iowa City, or as audiences of oral and written accounts of those who visited the IWP. Although most Chinese writers have learned about the American-style writing program exemplified by the IWW mostly through their encounters with the IWP, they have not erred too much by viewing the IWW and the IWP as something of a package deal.

The IWP and the IWW not only came from the same ideological and aesthetic origins, but throughout their histories, they also have both been deployed as tools of cultural diplomacy to inculcate the American way of viewing the world and spread the gospel of democracy across the globe.[1] More pertinent to the Chinese visitors, these two programs coalesced around the central cultural figures of Paul Engle and Hua-ling Nieh Engle. Paul Engle, one of the two cofounders of the IWP, served as director of the IWW for twenty-four years before stepping down in the 1960s, and he is still credited with raising the profile of the IWW from a regional powerhouse to an institution with national and international prominence. He also modeled the inner workings of the IWP on the IWW's design. Furthermore, he and his partner, Hua-ling Nieh Engle, the other cofounder of the IWP, deliberately cultivated close ties between the IWW and IWP from the very start. Paul Engle had been inviting international writers to the IWW since the 1950s. Upon founding the IWP, the couple also created "translation workshops" that called for collaboration between young, gifted American writers from the IWW and famous foreign writers who visited the IWP to produce first editions of foreign works in English. They initiated this arrangement so that the translation would not only be syntactically and idiomatically correct but also that it would have a tone that did not "reek of the translator's sweat."[2] This mode of engagement between domestic and international writers has stayed on at UI, and the Translation Workshop has evolved into a core offering of the current IWW curriculum.

Paul Engle claimed, "all the literatures of the world, in spite of their many-sounding languages, make one literature, for they all come from the same old imaginative expression of the gut-with-mind,"[3] but the language he chose to house this "one literature," as it turned out, was necessarily English. Seen in hindsight, Chinese intellectuals, when attempting to establish and uplift Chinese-language creative writing programs, are perhaps grappling with the central irony of adapting a model that privileges English as the universal language of communication and translation. But the literal, literary, and metaphorical translations that they undertook during their visits foreshadowed and shaped the ways they would execute the metaphorical translation project of founding Chinese writing programs based on a US model.

Recognizing that multiple sociopolitical, geopolitical, and personal factors have affected the emotional tones of Chinese writers' representations of their Iowa experiences, this chapter seeks to shed light on the ramifications of their *perceptions* of that fateful encounter rather than passing on their accounts as a complete picture of the IWP's role in Chinese writers' development or in world literature. Although sounding perhaps overly negative in some depictions, the majority of Chinese visitors did form warm personal relationships with their hosts. Yet the language barrier and cultural alienation can and have determined the quality of their experiences at the IWP. For visiting Chinese writers, to write, think, and interact with their environment and peers at the IWP is always "a cultural activity through which political meanings would be made," and this is this nowhere more apparent than in acts of translation.[4] Their interactions with their American hosts and writers from other countries influenced their understanding of their own identity, nation, and national literature and its relationship to the world and world literature. The concerns about their national literature and their own identity as writers often arose from and were expressed through issues related to language and translation. Even those who did not participate in a translation workshop to cotranslate their work into English must live the reality of "English as the singular, universal language" at the IWP.[5]

Translation functioned as a necessity for everyday living, a tool of communication, and, eventually, a foundation of identity during their residency. The Chinese visitors' experiences with translation at various levels and in multiple platforms provided by the IWP illustrate both the complex dynamics among individual writers and those between institutions such as the Chinese Writers' Association and the IWP. They also register generational differences and reveal—in both the Chinese visitors' subsequent and contemporaneous comments—not only an increasing awareness of the outside world but also a rising uneasiness among contemporary Chinese authors regarding the stature of China's literature in the world. Ultimately, the Chinese authors' tumultuous experiences at the IWP not only bring to the fore the hierarchy of languages and nations, which complicated both the relationships between them and their American hosts and the relationships among international writers, but they also yield clues to the founding of Chinese creative writing programs in an even more perilous twenty-first-century world.

Below, I investigate Chinese visitors' experiences in Iowa City and beyond as they are represented in published works such as diaries, literary essays, and news articles; archival materials, including unpublished scripts for public talks; and interviews of IWP staffers, including Hua-ling Nieh Engle. I argue that the Chinese visitors' intimate encounters with the IWP (and to a lesser extent, the IWW) have inspired them to develop as writers and future program founders even while posing unforeseen challenges to their sense of identity and security, not least because they were exposed not only to US culture but also to the international writing community in unprecedented ways. I first outline the IWP's selection process and programming for Chinese writers. In the next three sections, I examine the writers' depictions of their experiences as non-English speakers living and working in Iowa City and their impressions of the United States, focusing especially on the unique relationship between the mainland Chinese writer Wang Anyi and the Taiwan-based writer Chen Yingzhen 陈映真 (1937–2016). Finally, by sifting through their impressions of the IWP, Iowa City, and American culture, which was mediated by various agents, I explore how their intimate experiences of "English as a singular universal language" not only shaped their vision of Chinese literature and their identity as Chinese writers but also provided a model for Chinese writing programs in the future.

"Our Own Tower of Babel"

In *The World Comes to Iowa*, the IWP's twentieth-anniversary commemorative anthology published in 1987, Paul Engle tells a charming founding story. As he describes it, the idea came when he and Hua-ling Nieh were enjoying a leisurely boat ride on the Iowa River one summer evening in 1966. While he swam, she was cooking steaks and corn.

[With] the river turning green from its usual loam-gray as it flowed under the overhanging trees, the aroma of prime Iowa beef enriched with soy sauce, ginger, sherry, and green scallions, Hua-ling made the remark that changed not only our own lives from that day forward, but also, for the next twenty years, the lives of hundreds of foreign writers a world away whose names were yet unknown.[6]

Hua-ling asked Paul why they could not invite more international writers to UI, helping them the same way that the IWW had helped young American writers. This was no idle curiosity since Paul had directed the IWW from 1941 to 1965. Thanks to his commitment and hard work, the IWW became a national landmark for nurturing American talents in creative writing, and Iowa City became the only "City of Literature" in North America, awarded by UNESCO in 2008. In this account, however, Paul said he was shocked by Hua-ling's "crazy" idea initially. He raised various objections but eventually agreed to give it a try, provided that she help. They began to raise funds by tapping into private donors and federal agencies, and they invited writers from South Africa, Ireland, and East and West Germany during the first year of the IWP's founding.

The IWP's genesis under Paul Engle's pen, replete with evocative and prophetic details such as the fragrance of local corn and beef mingled with Chinese spices—a perfect union of Chinese and American ingredients—illustrates a vision of IWP as the embodiment of what Eric Bennett calls Engle's "internationalist cosmopolitanism."[7] Paul Engle describes the IWP as a peaceful oasis for the world's leading wordsmiths, who had become "endangered species" in their home countries: "To IWP come the world's horrors, fears, beauties, savagery, even triumphs, all at a level of intensity seldom known in the United States. The wounded come, scars invisible except in their eyes. For many, writing is not simply a career of words, but a matter of life or death." Fortunately, "In Iowa City, poets were and are free to speak, write, or sing about any subject or any person."[8] One cannot help but note his echo of "The New Colossus" by Emma Lazarus (1849–1887), engraved in the pedestal of the Statue of Liberty: "Give me your tired, your poor / Your huddled masses yearning to breathe free, / The wretched refuse of your teeming shore. / Send these, the homeless, tempest-tost to me."[9] To Paul Engle, the IWP did not merely provide networking opportunities. It also built "warm and trusting" relationships that transcended national or ethnic enmities: East and West German writers drank together; Israeli novelists invited a German poet to dinner; Japanese and Korean writers shared rice; and writers from mainland China and Taiwan met for the first time after thirty years of separation. Yet even while presenting the IWP as an exemplar of global integration, Engle's effort to depict international writers' experience of the IWP as "a neutral process free from political agitations" cannot completely mask its many tensions.[10]

Paul Engle, a highly regarded poet and charismatic leader, was also a bona fide cultural entrepreneur. Bennett, bestowing on him the epithet "a Creative Writing Cold Warrior," contends that Engle wielded the IWP as a tool of "soft diplomacy" for the US government.[11] The establishment of the IWP did not come from a spur-of-the-moment idea. As early as 1957, Engle had received funding from the Guggenheim Foundation to scout for artistic talent abroad. He was also supported by the US State Department to tour the world and attract authors to Iowa in the 1960s, during which period he met Hua-ling in Taiwan. His existing friendship with Averell Harriman, who became assistant secretary of state for Far Eastern affairs in 1961, also helped secure federal funding for the IWP.[12]

It is too hasty to conclude that Paul Engle's career was tainted by the suspicion of espionage because the IWP received funding from the Farfield Foundation, "a CIA front" by Bennett's characterization.[13] But Paul Engle did admit that funding came from "a curious combination of sources—the University of Iowa, the United States Information Agency (Office of International Visitors), many cultural affairs officers in U.S. embassies . . . corporations, foundations, and private individuals."[14] Even today, the IWP is funded by the US State Department for its various outreach cultural activities, such as theatre performances in China.[15] In its initial inception, it relied even more heavily on the support of the federal government, with Paul Engle as its chief spokesperson and extremely successful fundraiser.

Paul Engle directed the IWP at a time when American public attention shifted to domestic diversity rather than the tidal waves that were sweeping across the world. Nonetheless, the Engles claimed that the IWP not only provided refuge for persecuted foreign authors but also brought them together for the greater good of world literature and peace. Their goal to advance the humanistic spirit in the shadow of the USSR's totalitarian regime also contributed to the establishment of both an implicit language hierarchy that privileges English, and certain aesthetic standards as the only criteria for good literature, however. American-style creative writing programs taught aspiring authors these rules of propriety during the postwar period: Good literature contains sensations, not doctrines; experiences, not dogmas; memories, not philosophies. Their goal, according to Bennett, was to discourage the abstract theorizing and systematic social critiques typical of radical left-wing literature in favor of a focus on the personal, the concrete, and the individual. To avoid appearing to be imposing a particular ideology on writers like the communists were, program administrators like Engle presented these aesthetic principles as a nonpolitical, universally valid means of cultivating writerly craft.

While acknowledging that seemingly timeless criteria of good writing were inevitably historically bound, I also consider it crucial to study what role, if any, they play in defining world literature today. Many cultural institutions in the West, including the Nobel Prize Academy, value what Mads Rosendahl Thomsen calls "the literature of denial of life," which foregrounds matters of life, death, survival, trauma, and memory.[16] Although Paul Engel attributed the IWP's founding to serendipity, the selection criteria in the Engle era indicated a clear preference for writers who produced vivid renderings of personal experience of oppression and suffering, and the IWP's programming advanced their vision of nurturing such talent. As IWP alumna Wang Anyi puts it bluntly, the IWP seemed to be purposely looking for authors from "problem countries."[17]

This is not to deny that the founders' emphasis on Chinese authors' literary reputation and the social impact of their works back home—often at cross-purposes with the official position of English-language competency as a key criterion for selection adopted by US visa authorities—brought to Iowa City some of China's most famous writers.[18] The Engles were sometimes forced to defend their selection process to government agencies. In 1986, Hua-ling Engle categorically denied that the IWP had ever "nominated" any Chinese writers in a letter addressing concerns raised by USIA, the IWP's primary federal funding source. Decades later, however, she paints a more candid picture. She mentions that during the 1970s and 1980s, the IWP intentionally invited many Eastern European writers who faced oppression in their home countries, such as Vaclav Havel of the Czech Republic.[19] She also discloses that during her directorship of the IWP from 1978 to 1988, she selected Chinese writers based on her own judgment, assessing their impact in China but also showing special interest in those who had experienced "persecutions" from the party-state. "That made their works more interesting," she argues.[20]

Furthermore, IWP programing established by the Engles also reveals careful planning to realize their vision of promoting humanistic values in world literature. IWP visitors must fill out a form upon the completion of their residency, listing all the activities they have participated in. The Chinese alumni, usually helped by interpreters, gave public talks and seminars to discuss their writing careers and views on literature at UI and other US colleges and universities. The IWP provided instruction sheets with topics and prompts—including "Why I Write What I Write, and How I Write," "English Learned in Defiance," and "Images of America," among others—identifying areas of interest for the two hosts and the IWP's local American audiences undoubtedly while also showing the Engles' perception of the writers' lots in other countries.

In terms of execution, Paul Engle, aware of the participants' uneven language abilities, claimed that "translation goes on every day" in "our own Tower of Babel," a UI-owned dorm building named Mayflower.[21] Situated just north of campus, it faces a main road and the Iowa River, and it backs onto a thickly wooded hill. The international writers lived alongside six hundred students and shared living quarters with other IWP visitors in several small apartments on the eighth floor of one wing. Here, translation did indeed happen daily—literally, literarily, and metaphorically. Each pair of apartments is joined by a common kitchen and bath, an arrangement that "has been the occasional cause of some rancor but more often has led to good-natured adaptation and even close friendship among vastly different individuals from widely divergent cultures."[22] Rowena T. Torrevillas, a Filipino IWP alumna who was the daughter of a pair of 1946 alumni and who later on became administrative assistant at the IWP herself, roomed with the Chinese writer Chen Rong 谌容 in 1984. The two tried to communicate with each other using an English-Chinese dictionary, as Chen had just started learning English before leaving for the IWP.[23] Peter Nazareth, a writer of Malay and Indian descent who originally came from Uganda, also reminisces about his evolving roles as visiting writer, translator, and assistant director of the IWP. After his arrival at the IWP in 1973, he joined a working group organized by Hua-ling Engle and spent two years cotranslating literary works authored by Ding Ling 丁玲, Wang Meng 王蒙, and Liu Binyan 刘宾雁, the earliest visiting Chinese writers who would come to the IWP in the early 1980s. His translations later came out in the anthology *Literature of the Hundred Flowers*, edited by Hua-ling Nieh Engle and published by Columbia University Press in 1981.[24]

Nazareth did not know Chinese. That he had to work with John Hsu, a native speaker of Chinese, on the translation did not deter the Engles from recruiting him. Hua-ling Engle tapped him because he was a novelist and critic who expressed great interest in the ideology as well as the stories coming out of the Chinese Revolution. Paul Engle, in his typical expansive and poetic style, pushed for writers to be involved in literary translations because literature was "not written as a linguistic or scholarly exercise, but as an imaginative response of a living man to his lived life, expressing his shock or delight, his suspicion or praise." Lamenting the "actual death" of literary texts suffered at some translator's hand, he claimed that "the commonest cause of the fatality is linguistic competence without creative talent." He therefore advocated for "some imagination" to be mixed in with translations, and writers, with their capacity for imagination, would make ideal translators in his mind.[25]

In fact, the Engles themselves engaged in the substantial project of translating Mao Zedong's 毛泽东 poems from Chinese into English precisely at the same juncture when President Richard Nixon visited China in 1972, more than two decades after the founding of the People's Republic of China in 1949 led to the severing of diplomatic ties between the two governments. This move undoubtedly reflected the couple's political considerations on both national and institutional levels. Suggesting that Nixon present a copy of their translation to Mao as a gift, they sought to raise the profile of the IWP to the US federal government as an efficacious tool of cultural diplomacy, while signaling to the Chinese state their willingness to engage in cultural exchanges with mainland Chinese authors.

However, they also emphasized the value of translation to bring "common humanity" to life despite language barriers: "We were accustomed to searching for a common humanity and a common imagination in texts very strange to us. . . . All translations are a shadow cast by the live body of the original poem. The translator's job is to pump blood into the shadow. He never wholly brings it back to life, but he can make it breathe."[26]

The Engles promoted translations of foreign literature into English not merely to preserve and disseminate works by international writers, of course. As Engle predicted, "For the rest of the twentieth century, each country will have not one but two literatures: the one produced by its own writers, and the other translated from the world's languages. This secondary literature will often have the most immediate and energizing effect on writers of the language into which it has been translated."[27] That is to say, in his eye, English translations of foreign works would also electrify Anglophone writers. One can even argue that the Engles articulated translation in ways "that consolidate the US imperial power through the hegemony of English, at the same time becoming the agents of the authority who selected and compiled translated archives in English," since they chose foreign literary works worthy of translation and paired gifted American writers from the IWW with visiting international writers to form "cotranslation" teams.[28]

Seen in a broader context, the two cofounders of the IWP also engineered a metaphorical translation project to cultivate friendships and inculcate what they considered to be universal humanistic values among their international visitors by showing them the American way of life. Other than formal talks, seminars, and English classes, the Engles also offered up a rich array of extracurricular activities for all IWP visitors. These included outings to a local farm, allowing international writers to eat meals in a farm kitchen and ride on combines in soybean fields, and visits to the homes of Vachel Lindsay, Edgar Lee Masters, Mark Twain, and Abraham Lincoln, famous historical figures with local connections. The residency participants also went to concerts, plays, art exhibits, and dances, as well as to parties hosted by the Engles at their home in Iowa City. In 1979, the Engles organized a "Chinese Weekend" to welcome the first group of mainland Chinese writers to the IWP. To facilitate conversations between participants from the mainland and Taiwan, they arranged a boat ride on the Mississippi River, with bar food courtesy of John Deere, a major US manufacturer of farm machinery and one of the IWP's chief donors. This event claimed the national spotlight when it was reported in the *New York Times*, to the pride and delight of the Engles, who claimed their goal was to build bridges for estranged Sinophone writers across the Taiwan Strait or those who occupied different positions in the spectrum of the global Chinese diaspora, including those living in the US.[29]

As patrons of literature and capable administrators, the Engles undoubtedly devised these programs with an eye on a return for their investment. It was certainly useful to have international writers connect with donors, which showed American benefactors the results of their generosity. To hold public discussions and talks raised the profile of the IWP, while also familiarizing international visitors with local audiences, on whose good grace and collaboration—as well as their financial support—the IWP counted on. But more to the point, the goal for holding these "extracurricular" or "co-curricular" activities, as Paul Engle explained, was for the international writers not only to know each other better but also to "discover the United States." He promised that in Iowa, the writers would "get a feeling of the old America." By meeting with local residents, called by one writer "living memorials" and "the sort of men and women from whom Lincoln came," the visitors would "learn the true and gritty reality of this country."[30] How visiting Chinese writers thought of and responded to this kind of institutionalized hospitality, and what they gained from that experience, made for a story full of contradictions and ambiguities.

"The American Character"

The Chinese writers who visited the IWP between 1979 and 1989 arrived in Iowa City during a period fraught with tensions both at the IWP and in China. Compared to the Chinese IWP alumni of the twenty-first century, they were more freighted down by national and personal experiences during the Chinese revolutions of the twentieth century, especially the Cultural Revolution (1966–1976). Most of them also tended to evaluate their experiences at the IWP from a panoramic point of view and focus on the big picture of cultural rather than individual differences. The older authors also devised different strategies to deal with alienation than their younger colleagues did. While younger writers such as Wang Anyi expressed their anxieties more freely, their older colleagues often took refuge in portraying "the American character" as an outsider and observer, surreptitiously taking the moral and intellectual high ground that to some extent foreclosed more intimate engagements with the local culture. By elevating personal experiences to the plane of cultural critique, they reciprocated their hosts' eagerness to replace the Cold War rhetoric of rivalry and conflict with a vision of the harmonious unification of writers from the socialist and capitalist blocs, even as they wrote with equal measures of subversion and irony against the official line in reminiscent essays.

Starting in 1979, the IWP has invited two or three writers from mainland China annually, except for the years of 1990 and 1993, when only one visited, and the years of 1989, 1991, and between 1994 and 2000, when none came. These gaps can be attributed to a combination of factors. On the one hand, the Chinese Communist Party's (CCP) military crackdown on student demonstrations at the

Tian'an Men 天安门 Square in June 1989 and the ensuing international outcries and sanctions made such visits challenging to arrange if not completely impossible. On the other, the IWP was itself struggling for survival. After the retirements of Paul and Hua-ling Engle in 1977 and 1988 respectively, IWP leadership did not show the same level of energy, perseverance, and interest in China as the two cofounders had.[31] It also lacked stability. Turnover was high, with the directorship changing hands four times from 1988 to 1998, and a national search for a new director failed in 1999. The crisis came to a head when UI administration recommended closing the program, citing budget deficits in 1999. Not until May 2000, after Christopher Merrill was named director, did the IWP gradually find steady footing and begin to flourish again.

Across the Pacific Ocean, 1979 marked a turning point in the history of the PRC. Calling for economic reforms and the opening of China to the outside world after the Cultural Revolution had wreaked havoc on the national economy, education, and society for ten long years, the CCP started liberalizing the state-planned economy while relaxing its control in the cultural arena. Chinese writers subsequently began to reengage with the West after decades of isolation during the Cold War, ushering in a flood of foreign works and thoughts through translation, likened by some to the flooding of the Nile that brought rich nourishment to the (cultural) desert created by a ten-year draught. In contrast, 1989 represented the ending of a decade-long "honeymoon," during which mainland intellectuals had enjoyed increasing freedom of speech, government tolerance and support for a variety of literary and artistic experiments, and wider knowledge of, and recognition from, the international community. While the union between intellectuals and the party-state had always been fraught with ambiguity, the "Tian'an Men Incident" dealt liberal Chinese intellectuals a crushing blow, dispelling expressed and latent illusions and sending dissidents fleeing into exile abroad. That same year also saw the disintegration of the Soviet Union, the demolition of the Berlin Wall, and the official ending of the Cold War. The realignment of nations in ideological and geopolitical terms undoubtedly brought both shocks and inspirations to Chinese writers at the IWP and shaped their interactions with other visitors and the IWP staff between 1989 and 1999. The increasing market orientation of the Chinese economy, the loss of job security, and the tarnish of the cultural reputation of writers since 2000 would bring further changes to the content and form of their works, eventually leading them to teaching positions at writing programs at Chinese universities.

Several of the twenty-two writers who visited in the first decade following mainland Chinese writers' initial entry into the IWP in 1979 emerged from the New Culture Movement in China in the 1920s and 1930s, and they ranked among modern China's major literary figures: Xiao Qian 肖乾 (1979), Ai Qing

艾青 (1980), and Ding Ling (1981). Others, including Liu Binyan (1982), Ru Zhijuan 茹志鹃 (1983), Wang Meng (1987), and Bai Hua 白桦 (1988), entered China's literary scene around the time the PRC was founded in 1949, and they made a name for themselves before the Cultural Revolution erupted. Bei Dao 北岛 (1986) and Ah Cheng 阿城 (1986) represented "Misty Poetry" and "Roots-Seeking Literature" respectively, both experimental literary schools in the 1980s, while Wang Anyi, a rising young author when she visited the IWP, has continued to evolve and publish, and has, since the 1980s, gained increasing international recognition. Also worthy of note is that all these writers had suffered traumas during the Cultural Revolution, either by being persecuted as "rightist" or "anti-revolutionary" and indicted with an assortment of political crimes or by being exiled to rural areas to be "reeducated" as sent-down youths.

Representing different generations in modern Chinese literature, they had different degrees of exposure to world literature before arriving in Iowa. While in residence, they interacted in various ways with writers from other nations, the local community, and other US institutions of higher education. The language barrier presented a significant impediment to most Chinese writers during their residency, even though IWP staffers made sure that they were often accompanied by interpreters and that someone always drove them to shop for groceries weekly. Xiao Qian, a Cambridge-educated journalist who reported on World War II in Europe and visited the US in the 1940s, was fluent in English. Liu Binyan had passable English. Wang Meng studied English with the wife of a visiting Swedish author. Wang Anyi also took English classes at UI, which were specially arranged by the IWP for international visitors, with limited success. Feeling that they received "special treatment," however, made some visitors even more self-conscious, even though they appreciated their warm interactions with IWP staffers, especially the Engles, both at the time and later. In practical terms, their insufficient English limited their interactions with non-Chinese speakers, segregating them by the language they spoke and perhaps allowing them only superficial glances into American culture. Due to their limited language proficiency, navigating life in a "White" university town in the American Midwest, among international writers and alongside local Americans, brought unprecedented and unforeseen challenges to their personal, racial, and professional identities.

One is tempted to think that the mainland Chinese writers' experiences at the IWP would have been different had their mastery of English been on a par with their counterparts from Hong Kong and Taiwan, even though visitors from the three sites all experienced some form of cultural diplomacy that "consolidates the US imperial power through the hegemony of English."[32] The Hong Kong writer Gu Cangwu 古苍梧 was able to appropriate IWP resources to engage in grassroots political activism during his residency from 1970 to 1971. He coedited a newsletter produced in the IWP offices, participated in political demonstrations, and published correspondence in Hong Kong in support of the Baodiao 保钓 (Defending the Diaoyu Island) movement, which was seen as "a moment of unification within Chinese Diaspora, across national boundaries and political alliances briefly, and based on a Western model of political democracy."[33] The example of Chen Yingzhen, who visited the IWP in 1983, further shows how English language skills not only enabled him to render invaluable help to Hua-ling Engle and other visiting foreign writers but also to build a bridge between writers across the Taiwan Strait, especially through his recounting of fellow international writers' stories in Chinese to Wang Anyi and her mother, Ru Zhijuan.

Yet despite language barriers and a relatively short stay in Iowa City for roughly two months, the mainland Chinese writers who visited from 1979-1989 have left behind ample literary records of their IWP experiences, far more than those who came from China in the following decades. This is partly thanks to the high profile and high impact of the IWP at the time. An internationally acclaimed program that provided one of the rare and earliest opportunities for Chinese writers to reengage with the West after thirty years of isolation, it also roused attention from the two national governments and put them on high alert, as both viewed the program as a form of soft power. Partly, this is also because the visiting Chinese writers, a group of self-conscious "chosen few" who survived national and personal traumas to eventually visit the US, a perpetual source of both attraction and repulsion for the Chinese imaginary, felt the burden of history and an urgent sense of mission. The visiting Chinese authors did enjoy their stay at the IWP in many ways. It offered a much-needed reprieve from constant political struggles and state surveillance, and in addition to exchange opportunities, it also gave them time to complete their projects. Wure Ertu 乌热尔图 savored "the great sense of flexibility" and love for "variability and pluralism" in Iowa City, without feeling afraid to be the first victim to be "shot down from the horseback" in any political movement by people who loved to "try their knives on the writers" back home.[34] Wang Meng drafted his novel *Dapple* at the IWP, and Chen Baichen 陈白尘 finished a memoir about his experience during the Cultural Revolution while he was there. But the sharp contrast between the past and the present, and the unmistakable inklings of seismic domestic and global changes ahead, also compelled them to ponder the fate of their nation and its national literature as well as their identities.

The Chinese writers wrote both to respond to the expectations of their Chinese and US sponsors and to reflect on their own experiences, inevitably revealing not only the dynamics at IWP but also the lingering effects of their "past life" prior to the visit. Most wrote short literary essays reminiscing about their IWP residency. The one exception thus far is the book-length treatment *Munü manyou Meilijian* 母女漫游美利坚, or *Mother and Daughter Toured the USA*, coauthored by the mother-daughter team of Ru Zhijuan and Wang Anyi, who visited the IWP together in 1983. Most of the essays describe out-of-town trips organized by the IWP. Only a few, such as those authored by Ding Ling, Xiao Qian, Wang Meng, and Liu Binyan, all some of the earliest visitors, depict and comment on their experiences in Iowa City. Some authors offer glowing reportage about the American spirit and ostensibly call for the Chinese to catch up, but they also offer subtle counternarratives within the same piece or in their writings elsewhere. For instance, Ding Ling ends the description of her first experience of an American football game with a eulogy of the American national character: "The strength, the joy, and the zeal are so typical of the American people's energy: brave as a lion and persistent as an eagle. . . . These are optimistic and wholesome people. They know how to live."[35] However, this complimentary ending contrasts sharply with her bewilderment and helplessness throughout the game, a feeling shared by a Hungarian couple and an Indian couple the Engles also took to the game. Faced with obtuse game rules and deafening cheering from a crowd of one hundred thousand spectators, twice the size of the population of Iowa City, Ding Ling felt lost, "like a kernel of corn floating on a sea of people," and the Indian woman looked "like a fragile reed in the wind" against the large Americans sandwiching her.[36] Ding Ling was nevertheless able to bond with the Hungarian writer and his spouse over a shared love of ping-pong, with her saying in Chinese the names of famous players from China and Hungary. One cannot help noticing her strategic move of countering a quintessential American sport with one that Chinese athletes excelled in and that was wielded as a tool of cultural diplomacy by the Chinese government in their attempts to normalize relations with the US and other Western countries at the time. The irony cannot be lost on the reader, either, when she flexes Chinese cultural muscles and claims solidarity with a writer from another socialist nation, all while attending an event arranged by her IWP hosts to show off American culture and power.

We can detect a similar pattern of simultaneous cooperation with and challenge to the discourses of harmony and collaboration propagated by both the IWP and the Chinese state in other recollections. Xiao Qian, after talking with some bartending UI students, concludes, "Young Americans are proud of being self-reliant and are reluctant to depend on their parents for money,"[37] which proves to be a far cry from his criticism of American social ills when he was covering the launch of the United Nations in 1946.[38] Xiao was understandably being cautious. Selected by the Engles as the first mainland Chinese writer to visit the IWP, and summoned by the Chinese Writers' Association mere months after he was rehabilitated following a twenty-year exile as a "rightist," he was tasked with using this trip "to make friends for my country and to dispel misunderstanding . . . without saying an improper word."[39] Xiao later admitted to having ceded all decision-making to Bi Shuowang 毕硕望, a high official in the Chinese Writers'

Association who accompanied him and acted as his "minder" while they visited the IWP in 1979.

Xiao was also aware of his American host's interests. In 1979, the IWP hoped to make a statement as the first US cultural institution to invite a mainland Chinese writer to visit, and they needed a "presentable" specimen. Years later, Hua-ling Engle explained that she selected Xiao because of his educational and work experiences in the West: he could speak English, he knew how to interact with English-speaking audiences, and he was always all smiles.[40] Their confidence in Xiao was apparently amply rewarded. His "Revelations of Iowa" was published in *People's Daily*, a party organ, with a copy sent to USIA by Paul Engle as proof of the IWP's role in propagating a positive American image among the Chinese. Engle asserts, "The story was read in every city and town in China. . . . It is a breakthrough also for the USA; our Embassy could not plant so favorable a story. This shows the tremendous power of the written word to reach into the corners of a great country and the world influence of this Program [IWP]."[41] Yet one cannot help marveling at how much Xiao changed from the position he expressed in "Some Judgments of America." An essay first written in Chinese in the 1940s and translated and republished in 1989, it describes prevalent racism in the US and includes Xiao's critique of the "impetuous" American national character arising from a sense of entitlement thanks to rich natural resources, incidentally foreshadowing Wang Anyi's similar observations in 1983.[42]

Other than the intentionally or unintentionally ironical accounts of the American character they produced, equally telling were the alliances and friendships the visiting Chinese writers formed while visiting the IWP. Irrespective of Paul Engle's idyllic depiction of authors coming together and transcending historical and contemporary racial and national animosities, the Chinese visitors formed deeper and more meaningful bonds with those who shared their ethnicity, language, or the collective experience of living under a communist regime or in a "third-world" country. Wang Meng found Chinese-speaking visitors from Taiwan and Chinese Americans "not at all foreign," chatted in Uyghur with a Turkish poet, and "toasted the friendship between the Chinese and Romanians and shared the concern over the events in Poland" with a Romanian author, in English no less.[43] His experience dovetails with Wang Anyi's observation as well. As she testifies, at the IWP, authors "from the Socialist bloc were all friendly toward one another."[44]

"Lost in Translation"

Of all the portrayals of Chinese writers' experiences at the IWP, *Mother and Daughter Toured the USA* stands out the most. It not only gives the IWP residency the full treatment it deserves but also marks a gradual generational shift to more individualistic concerns among visiting Chinese writers while presenting a more candid portrait and commentary of the famed American-style writing program. Split into two parts, it features two diaries, the first by Ru Zhijuan and the second by Wang Anyi, in their totality. It purportedly records their day-to-day experiences in the US from September to December 1983, though they spent only the first two months at the IWP. The entries cover about one hundred days, describing in detail domestic chores such as cooking, cleaning, and shopping, as well as public events such as talks and group outings. This book, originally published in 1986, was reissued in 2018 under a slightly different title to commemorate the twentieth anniversary of Ru Zhijuan's passing in 1998. It also provided Wang Anyi with the opportunity to look back on that experience and reflect on her "immature" and frequently insecure younger self engaged in constant argument and struggle with her mother while at the IWP, though she insisted that she rendered an honest account despite her diary's obvious shortcomings of being "lengthy, haphazard, petty, and boring."[45]

Chinese authors undoubtedly felt a greater sense of freedom after decades of political campaigns and censorship back home. Wure Ertu, for instance, told his audience at the Images in America seminar in 1986: "Somebody told me before I came here that if I don't speak English, I'll be like a dummy. I do feel this way, but I am a happy dummy here."[46] But in the diary, Wang Anyi does not share his sanguineness about the linguistic deficiency, even though she also enjoys the beautiful natural scenery and vibrant cultural life in Iowa City. For her, the language barrier and the hierarchy it represents remain painfully real. Above all, she feels a deep sense of loss in an alien world. Words like "dream," "unreal," "misty," or "dazed" (huanghu 恍惚) appear frequently in her diary. Both Ru and Wang also describe repeated incidents of losing their way. Even though the route seems straightforward in hindsight, Wang is often afraid that she cannot find her way back to Mayflower when going out on her own. She muses, "This is a world too alien to me. It is so easy to lose self-confidence here."[47] Losing one's way is a perfect metaphor, for she could never feel at home at the IWP, admitting, "It feels unreal and misty forever, because it belongs to others."[48]

Wang feels at once drawn to and alienated by the pervasive American affluence and cheerfulness around her, which she appreciates but also fears will spotlight her own inadequacy. She describes in loving detail the scents, sounds, and colors of the local Old Capital Mall, where she went browsing frequently. Yet three separate times she postpones buying a coveted coat due to financial concerns. The Japanese writer and 2003 IWP alumna Minae Mizumura comments that "traveling in a foreign country for even a week makes you painfully aware of the economic status of your own country. Living in a foreign country for an entire month with people from a wide spectrum of rich countries to poor sharpens your awareness even more."[49] Mizumura could afford luxuries such as afternoon drinks at local bars, where she socialized with writers from other "rich countries," while those in financial straits had to economize on food to send their stipends home. The Chinese writers similarly socialized only among themselves and with people from similar socioeconomic strata. They were scrupulous about what dishes to contribute to potlucks and about borrowing even a cup of rice from a neighbor.[50]

Wang Anyi admires Iowa's rich black soil, tidy farmhouses, and content local farmers contrasted sharply with flashbacks of her experience in China's rural Anhui province as an "educated youth," where she encountered poverty and hardship everywhere she went. She observes that local residents like to fly a national flag in their yard for no special reason other than to express "patriotism" or satisfaction with life in general.[51] In hindsight, she considers it a revelation of "American Exceptionalism," or a national sense of entitlement that comes with blessed lives, contrasted with the struggles experienced by other nations and peoples.[52] But her first visit to the US generated more senses of inferiority than clear-sighted analyses.

She later admits that she had a chip on her shoulder (*daizhe yuan* 带着怨) when visiting the IWP.[53] Still mourning the ravages caused by the Cultural Revolution, she shared her generation's anger about wasted youth, inadequate schooling, and the chaos in a transitional Chinese society. She had returned to Shanghai in 1978 after spending several years in the countryside, and she arrived in Iowa City in 1983, not yet thirty. She was emerging as a promising young talent when her short story "Ben ci lieche zhongdian" 本次列车终点站 ("The Final Destination of this Train") won a prestigious national literary prize—"Excellent Chinese Short Stories of the Year"—in 1981. It was later translated into English as "The Destination" and published in *Chinese Literature*, the only state-sponsored Chinese journal to introduce translations of Chinese works to the world. However, as a young author still finding her own voice, and secretly afraid her invitation to the IWP came from her association with her mother rather than on her own merit, she lacked the self-assurance (and perhaps also the emotional moderation) of older generations of established authors such as her mother Ru Zhijuan, Ding Ling, and Xiao Qian.[54] Her diffidence was further exacerbated by her limited language skills. She wished to have her work critiqued at the IWW, but the students and professors there showed no interest after reading the English translations of her short stories "Life in a Small Courtyard" and "The Destination." Published in the state-run *Chinese Literature*, the English translations perhaps had not done justice to her works. But she felt hurt by perceived rejections by her American peers: "I don't think that my work cannot live up to their standards. . . . I feel that people here don't really desire to know us, but only want to show themselves to us all the time."[55] She also noted that IWW members never attended any IWP events.[56] When her desire to interact with local writers was not reciprocated, she again became defensive: "I do not wish to prove myself here. I only want to understand them more."[57] When the Hong Kong writer Pan Yaoming (Pun Yiu-Ming) 潘耀明 states that diplomas were rated high in the US, she broods, "Those I don't have. I only have my fiction. But they don't understand my fiction. They only acknowledge English works," a comment that also reveals differences in life experience and worldview among Sinophone writers based in mainland China, Hong Kong, and Taiwan.[58]

Wang's sense of injury induces reactions in her that are distinct from those of her mother, even when they look at the same event. Describing the same seminar featuring Chinese writers, Wang and Ru arrive at quite different conclusions. While Ru expresses an appreciation for the intimate setting and courtesy shown by the thirty-some attendees, most of them Chinese students or scholars, Wang feels disappointed about the small size of the audience.[59] Although Hua-ling Nieh Engle assures her that it had been the best seminar held by Chinese writers in recent years, she was not convinced. She feels that the audience is indifferent, "as if people did not understand and did not wish to understand us."[60] Whereas the lack of public adulation presented a cultural shock to Wang in 1983, Chinese authors visiting the IWP years later, such as Ge Fei 格非, interpreted it as an indication of "the decline of literature all over the world."[61]

The mother and daughter also devised different strategies to handle a sense of alienation. Ru comments on the polite hypocrisy of White salesclerks serving non-White clients, and the implicit racism in the US, like "a smiling, polite, and soft net" that segregated racial and ethnic groups.[62] Her way of asserting cultural superiority, though invariably understated, lies in criticizing American foodways: pots and pans have no lids, factory-raised chickens taste like nothing, the American signature dish of steak is more hype than substance, and even Engle's hospital meal could never compare with Ba Jin's 巴金 in Shanghai.[63] In contrast, Wang finds solace in Black music, such as the jazz concert she heard in Chicago. As if seeing "the first slave boat out of Africa and the first group of enslaved people," she asserts, "it was not a performance of skills but that of the heart."[64]

Other than sampling music expressing enslaved people's sufferings, Wang also deploys psychological and verbal overcompensation to counter American audiences' perceived apathy toward Chinese literature. She appears very sensitive to criticisms of Chinese art and the Chinese nation, even while noting the shortcomings of both. After the screening of *Xi'an shibian* 西安事变 (*The Xi'an Incident*) at UI, she feels offended that the American audience complained of its length.[65] When another Chinese film, *Chengnan jiushi* 城南旧事 (*Old Stories in South Beijing*) is better received, she comments, "We have a motherland that causes us heartaches. . . . Whether right or wrong, it is ours. There is only one Beijing, and only one China. If you want it, take it all. If not, there would be nothing left."[66]

Rather than eulogizing about the idyllic IWP, as Ding Ling and Xiao Qian did, she also notices many problems among fellow writers: poverty, alcoholism, mental health issues, racy language, inappropriate behavior, and one arrest for petty theft.[67] She feels unhappy when she is told by her interpreter, a work-study student from Taiwan, that the IWP sought out writers from the "Third World," perhaps resenting being lumped into a category that not only wiped out national and individual differences but also codified the inferiority of the "Third World."[68] Although she joins other international visitors at public events, such as a panel on women writers' experiences in different countries, descriptions of those remain desultory in her diary. She writes little on spending much leisure time with non-Chinese speakers as well, though she occasionally joins in the noisy parties at Mayflower. She apparently feels their self-abandoned way of partying highlights her lacking: "These weekends make me feel that I have never enjoyed myself to my heart's content during the first half of my life."[69]

Faced with perceived indifference from an alien world, Wang interacted with Chinese speakers the most. Whether from Taiwan, Hong Kong, Malaysia, Korea, or mainland China, the Chinese speakers shopped, drank, ate, traveled, and partied together. She even found a common song to sing along with them: "*Long de chuanren*" 龙的传人 (Progeny of the Dragon). A historic cultural artifact, the song was composed by Taiwan artist Hou Dejian 侯德健, sung by Hong Kong singer Zhang Mingmin 张明敏 at the Chinese New Year's Variety Show in 1983, and broadcast by the Chinese Central TV station to promote the unification of all ethnic Chinese across national borders. Endorsing the connective power of shared cultural inheritance, Wang enjoyed warm relationships with fellow writers from Taiwan and Hong Kong. Differences of opinion on what counted as good art presented opportunities for further exchanges. Critiques of the others' films about life on the opposite side of the Taiwan Strait made for lighthearted bantering. An occasional sparring over what "the collective" meant highlighted their different upbringings but did no damage to friendships. Even the celebration of China's National Day on October 1, an event that could potentially bode ill for attendees from Taiwan if the Guomindang 国民党 (GMD) government got wind of their "treasonous act," saw them united at the same table with a potluck dinner and much wine.

The Mentor and the Recalcitrant Pupil

Wang formed a special friendship with Taiwan writer Chen Yingzhen at the IWP. After serving his sentence for alleged political crimes in Taiwan, Chen was finally able to visit the IWP after the initial invitation from the Engles was annulled due to his imprisonment by the GMD in 1969. Fluent in English, he delivered talks and acted as an interpreter for other Chinese-speaking visitors. He also worked as an unofficial assistant to Hua-ling Nieh Engle to help her host Chinese writers, planning out itineraries and taking care of logistical details. Chen expressed the most concern, curiosity, and appreciation about Wang out of all the mainland Chinese writers he met at the IWP in 1983.[70] Chen praised Wang's "seriousness and sincerity" seen in her works. He not only read all her books gifted by her, but also published Wang's short story, "The Destination," in *Wenji* 文季 (*Season of Literature*), an influential literary journal in Taiwan in 1984; it was likely the first instance of a Taiwan literary journal publishing work by a mainland Chinese author.

On November 15, 1983, Wang wrote, "This is the most precious page. World should be like this, with friends together, compatriots together, and family together. But I cannot write about it at the moment. Well, I won't write about it, but I will keep it all in my heart. I think I can write about what the world ought to be like one day."[71] She was alluding to bidding farewell to Chen and his wife before they departed the next day, apparently moved to incoherence or perhaps out of discretion. In contrast, her mother, in her entry for the same day, only noted the event with a simple sentence: "Some compatriots came to say goodbye."[72] Chen Yingzhen's influence on Wang Anyi would gradually come to light in the decades after they parted ways in 1983. Wang has not only described their initial interactions at the IWP, but she has also repeatedly reflected upon that period and written at least two pieces to commemorate their relationship: "Wutuobang shipian" 乌托邦诗篇 (Utopian Verses, 1991) and "Yingtenaxiongnaier" 英特纳雄耐尔 (International, 2003), with the latter being published twenty years after their first meeting.

What exactly is the nature and extent of Chen's influence on Wang? Above all, Chen represented cultural and moral authority and stood in as a father figure for a younger writer who was still honing her craft and seeking recognition. At the IWP, Wang highly valued Chen's opinions and craved his approval. When she mentioned that she was taking English classes, and that she felt learning a foreign language would "open one more window onto the world," Chen applauded her effort. When she commented that works by Taiwan writers focused too narrowly on their own private lives without addressing larger crises in society, he praised her acumen. It was no small thing for a young writer unsure about her position at the IWP and in the world to receive validation by her "idol." To Wang, Chen was not just an older famous writer who served as a father figure and who made up for the absence of her biological father at key moments in her life.[73] He also spoke from a position of righteousness and moral authority. Whether agreeing with his promotion of literature's social impact, Wang admired Chen's ethical code. The Engles had offered to employ an American attorney to secure his release from prison in Taiwan when Chen was incarcerated earlier. But Chen and his father declined, stating that Chinese problems should be handled by the Chinese alone, an act that Wang believed manifested loyalty to one's race and culture.[74] She also found Chen's example inspiring because his strong faith in Christianity and in socialism set up a sharp contrast to what she saw as the "lack of belief" in her own generation, even as she aligned herself with those disillusioned by the Cultural Revolution despite, or precisely because of, their earlier infatuation with and unquestioning subscription to Maoism.

Furthermore, Wang looked to Chen for a "redemptive" force that could lift her above material experiences and ascend to the realm of profound spiritual awakening. As she intones in "Utopian Verses," reminiscing about him provides her with "a comfort, an ideal," "a pure land to preserve pure, good, and beautiful things," and the "help" to transcend the chaotic multitudes of reality and look toward "a splendid world hidden behind clouds." The recollection of him also works as "romantic love" (aiqing 爱情), making her work harder to perfect herself under a pair of eyes that only exist in her mind. Yet neither lavish attention from such a much-admired authority figure at the time nor lingering yearning for his "Godlike love" converted Wang to Chen's vision of literature.

In her own words, Chen's influence has worked like a "grindstone." She claims that at the IWP, he steered her away from excessive materialism and consumerism and hence saved her from falling prey to the seduction of capitalism.[75] Almost a decade after the IWP, she also admitted that as a young and stubborn writer lacking in self-confidence but unwilling to admit her own insecurity, she used Chen's opinion as "a spur" (quce 驱策) to force herself out of her comfort zone.[76] She had made a name for herself as a "realist" young writer with works such as the novel *Junior High Graduates, Class of '69* (69 jie chuzhong biyesheng 六九届初中毕业生) after being trained at the prestigious Central Writers' Institute (Zhongyang Wenxue Jiangxi Suo 中央文学讲习所) in Beijing in 1980, an experience characterized by her as one of the two key moments in her writing career.[77] It was grueling to abandon her earlier success in producing award-winning works based on her experience growing up in China in the 1950s and 1960s. She felt she must break free from prior training and experience and remake herself as a writer. In fact, Wang suffered a serious writer's block that lasted several years after her residency at the IWP, until she broke through to embark on a "metatextual turn" in her writing career.[78]

Still, Wang credits her IWP residency as the other key moment that shaped her writing, claiming that her experience in Iowa City expanded her horizons considerably.[79] Chen Yingzhen contributed to this writerly "rebirth." In terms of both Chinese and global politics, 1983 was an eventful year. A South Korean passenger jet was "accidentally" shot down by a USSR missile, causing an uproar among visiting writers from the socialist bloc. Additionally, the date of Hong Kong's handover to China was decided, sending shockwaves across the stock market in Hong Kong, much to the dismay of the visiting Hong Kong writer Pan Yaoming. Against this background, Chen taught her to look at her own problems in the context of the whole world.[80] Thanks to his good English, he was able to recount to Wang the various tragedies experienced by the other visiting international writers, and he convinced Wang that everyone at the IWP had suffered personal, racial, and national traumas. His own personal experience and ethical practice undoubtedly also remained an implicit yet forceful tool of persuasion. Wang recalls that Chen got impatient with her after hearing so many of her complaints about the wreckage caused by the Cultural Revolution. Chen challenged her to show something different through her work rather than wallowing in perceived victimization since there were so many unimaginable sufferings all over the world. Wang Anyi did learn to shake off the shadow of the Cultural Revolution and examine the problems of China and her generation in a larger context, but it took time and a turn toward a market economy in China to alert her to the full ramifications of capitalism. At the IWP, the two of them got into heated arguments as Chen attempted to steer her away from individual concerns that were too narrowly defined.[81] Wang accepted Chen's criticism with more equanimity than she did receiving it from her mother, partly because there were no complicated family dynamics getting in the way and partly out of appreciation for his attention. Otherwise, the two of them remained apart in terms of their ideological positions, writing styles, and views on the function of literature.

Chen remained steadfast in his lifelong denunciation of the evils of capitalism and his sympathy for lower-class people, regarding literature as a tool of social engineering and intervention, whether it was during the time when he resided in Taiwan or after his relocation to mainland China. Indeed, he introduced the concept of "Third World Literature" to Taiwan beginning in the mid 1980s after his encounter with writers not only from mainland China but also from South Africa, the Philippines, and Eastern Europe at the IWP.[82] In contrast, Wang has turned farther and farther away from socialist-realist themes in her works while tacitly acknowledging the limits of literature to effect social change, though she did come to accept Chen's critique of capitalism. At the IWP, Chen once accused her of opposing her mother, Ru Zhijuan, "for the sake of opposition," yet Wang criticized Ru's works as being "too ideological" even more than a decade later, which is consistent with her critique of Chinese literature of the "socialist-realist" stripe in general.[83]

Po-hsi Chen asserts that Chen's socialist ideals and his religious faith "provided Wang with a concentric framework to first position China and Chinese literature within a worldly context, and next, within the concept of utopian idealism."[84] Yet Wang's take on "utopian idealism" rests in its failure and the resulting disillusionment. Not only did she fail to follow in Chen's footsteps to write literature that was more socially aware, but she also reconciled with Chen only through the acknowledgement of their shared tragic fate as writers. Two decades later, in her final recollection of Chen Yingzhen in "International," Wang opines that Chen gave up writing fiction because he lost confidence in literature's ability to "convey reality" (*chengzai xianshi* 承载现实). In noting the father figure's "weakness" (*canruo* 孱弱) and childlike willfulness (*renxing* 任性), Wang recognizes both her own maturation and their common destiny: betrayed by utopian idealism, left behind by the tides of times, bewildered by the dizzying changes in the consumerist contemporary world, and yet ultimately unable to articulate what they really wish for. Chen answered the call of communism and moved to mainland China, while Wang mostly embraced the tenets of artistic freedom and individualism in writing in the two decades after they first met in Iowa City. "I pursued him for twenty years but was only infected by his disappointment. . . . I was never able to catch up with him, but he was also left behind by the times," Wang stated in 2003.[85] In the end, the mentor and pupil were reunited on a platform of discontent, equally disillusioned by their respective earlier ideals, though equally adamant in rejecting what they considered anathema to their values.

Despite all the vicissitudes in their respective lives, and even as Wang grew into an internationally renowned, award-winning writer, she feels she owes a debt of gratitude to Chen and still values his opinion. She laments that she was "misunderstood" by Chen as someone interested only in writing nostalgic tales of old Shanghai without taking up "more important and greater [humanistic] concerns."[86] She also regards the fact that they were awarded "Huazong shijie huayu wenxue jiang" 花踪世界华语文学奖 (Huazong Prize in Sinophone Literature)—a biennial literary prize sponsored by the Malaysia-based *Sin Chew Daily* 星洲日报—back to back in 2001 and 2003 as a way to acknowledge and reciprocate Chen's mentorship twenty years earlier.[87] She had in fact nominated Chen for the award after hearing about his financial difficulties after his move to mainland China, and she wrote "International" as her speech at the award ceremony.

Found in Translation

Wang Anyi's relationship with Chen Yingzhen illustrates that what the visiting Chinese writers have gained from their IWP experiences cannot be quantified or qualified within the mere perimeters of a two-month residency, and it must instead be investigated through longitudinal studies. However, even where recollections are brief and incomplete, we can ascertain that the Chinese alumni's exposure to the international writing community and US culture at the IWP—with all the human frailties and vagaries of life that it entailed—has left a significant and lasting impact. Their interactions with colleagues from other countries, the

US or otherwise, sharpened their sense of the intricate relationships between world literature, international politics, and self-image. The legacy of their IWP experiences, as we shall see throughout the remainder of this book, has been captured not just in their IWP reminiscences, but also in subsequent creative works and the Chinese writing programs that they have helped to build, modeling on the IWW and the IWP.

Wang Anyi launched the Shanghai Writing Program (Shanghai Xiezuo Jihua 上海写作计划) in 2008, and she cofounded Fudan University's MFA in creative writing in 2009. The Shanghai Writing Program annually invites selected international writers to reside in Shanghai from September 1 to October 31 to "experience Shanghai like a native." Following the design of the IWP, though on a smaller scale, visiting writers are expected to engage in exchanges with Shanghai-based writers, as well as with faculty and students of institutions of higher education, while also giving readings and public talks.[88] In a similar vein, the Chinese Writers' Association has established the Lushan International Writing Camp (Lushan Guoji Xiezuo Ying 庐山国际写作营). Hong Kong Baptist University has created their own International Writers' Workshop (Guoji Zuojia Gongzuofang 国际作家工作坊) and in January 2023, it launched a bilingual MA program in Chinese- and English-language creative writing.

Undergirding such programs were Chinese writers' considerations of language hierarchy, translation, and the fate of Chinese literature in the world, mediated by cultural conduits such as Chen Yingzhen and the IWP staffers. When visiting the IWP for the first time, Wang Anyi argued, "We come from so many different countries. Why is only English recognized as the common language [at the IWP]?"[89] After hearing a talk comparing Chinese and Western poetry by Professor William Yip at UC San Diego, she further lamented, "These two cultures are very hard to communicate and interact with each other."[90] Wang's concern about, and challenge to, the hegemony of the English language remains relevant even today. Later visitors to the IWP, such as the Chinese novelist Bi Feiyu 毕飞宇, also see Chinese literature as "disadvantaged" (*ruoshi* 弱势) given its limited influence abroad—despite the Nobel Prize in Literature awarded to Mo Yan—contending that the slow process of translation presents a major obstacle to Chinese literature's outreach to the world. Even though he claims he had no "nationalist consciousness" (*guozu yishi* 国族意识), he asserts that the more attention China attracts from the world as a country, the more interest Chinese literature will generate among international audiences.[91] Ge Fei also contends that Europeans and Americans, not Chinese, can speak from a position of self-perceived "cultural superiority" and define "how to interpret and judge literature."[92]

The concern with the stature of a particular national literature in the world is of course not limited to Chinese writers. Mizumura, for one, notes that, judging by the number of people who speak it as a second language, English has become the singular universal language and is threatening to swallow up other national literatures in the age of the internet.[93] Making Chinese writers' anxieties surrounding this issue all the more acute, in recent years, some Western Sinologists (though not all of them), such as Wolfgang Kubin, have purportedly dismissed contemporary Chinese novels as "trash." Howard Goldblatt, who is the principal translator of Mo Yan's works into English and who has been credited with propelling Mo's ascent to winning the Nobel Prize in Literature, was also reported to have associated the failure of modern Chinese literature to "step into the world" with the lack of psychological depth in contemporary Chinese novels.[94]

The Chinese state, local media, and social media played a role in stirring up nationalist fervor by sensationalizing Western scholars' alleged denigration of Chinese literature. But such reports have made a significant impact. According to Deng Changliang, the negative assessments of Chinese literature from abroad have generated bifurcated positions of eulogizing or condemning contemporary Chinese literature among Chinese intellectuals in recent years, a trend that can also be seen in my interviews with faculty members at Chinese writing programs (see the introduction).[95] But the visiting Chinese writers' difficulties in making themselves (literally) understood and their works appreciated by foreign audiences in the purportedly cosmopolitan setting of the IWP already foretold Chinese writers' and scholars' struggles with existing linguistic and cultural hierarchies today. Not surprisingly, Chinese writers welcome the opportunity to "step into" world literature with the help of translation. Yet if translation provides the only route to world literature, it also raises a host of complex issues related to ideological, cultural, and national contestations. David Damrosch famously asserts that "world literature is writing that gains in translation."[96] In his article "Mapping Chinese Literature as World Literature," Yingjin Zhang argues, however, that Damrosch's definition could be modified to, "World literature is writing that gains in translation when it is done in English or another major European language,"[97] given the dominant "technologies of recognition" in the West.[98] Moreover, Zhang asserts, any apparent loss of "aura" after translation into English should not automatically diminish the value of the original work, since untranslatability may have more to do with culture than with language,[99] as is demonstrated by the case of Zhang Ailing's fiction.[100]

Furthermore, it was not only the dominance of English but also certain aesthetic standards taken for granted by the Engles and their Western colleagues that presented potential hurdles to Chinese literature's entry into world literature. After Chen Rong delivered a talk at the University of Nebraska in 1984, Professor Frederick M. Link, chair of the English Department, wrote to praise her work: "Two aspects of your work interest me especially. One is its moral fervor; the conviction that literature can be a significant force in a culture. . . . The other difference is that you are not afraid of storytelling and seem to be writing for some public broader than other writers and literary critics." While noting the contrast between socially aware and outward-oriented Chinese literature of the 1980s, and modern American literature "devoted to demonstrating in ever more elliptical ways the technical virtuosity of the writer . . . , an exercise in solipsism," he also criticizes the "heavy and clumsy" English translation of Chen Rong's novella.[101] Link's letter shows that the language barrier can be reinforced not merely by inadequate translation, from which Chinese authors, rightly or wrongly, feel their works frequently suffer. Some Chinese works were patently harder to translate into English than others, as can be seen in Wendy Larson's complaint to the IWP about the "opaque" prose typical of the fiction by Can Xue 残雪, an avant-garde Chinese writer known for her experimental works.[102] Different aesthetic criteria also impede Chinese writers from stepping onto the world stage. For example, both Link and Goldblatt note that Chinese writers privilege storytelling more than artistic form or psychological depth of character. Yet Link views it a welcome contrast to American writers' narcissistic fixation on craft, while Goldblatt considers it a fatal flaw of contemporary Chinese novels.

Today, English still dominates as the language of global communication and translation, while certain Western-centric "universal" criteria of good writing continue to inform the definition of literature worthy of global recognition. Meanwhile, Chinese writers and intellectuals are enthusiastically pursuing the project of building creative writing programs at Chinese universities based on their experiences with the American-style writing programs. At the same time, they have consciously or unconsciously changed their writing styles, arguably to make their works more translatable and thereby more accessible to Western audiences. Deng Rubing observes a change of tone in talks given by Chinese writers visiting the IWP before and after the turn of the twenty-first century, as they moved away from "collectivist" to more "individualist" mindsets. Their writing styles have also shifted in recent years. Ge Fei, previously known for his experimental, avant-garde writing style in the 1990s, turned to more traditional ways of storytelling after visiting the IWP in 2009. Nowadays, he promotes a kind of Chinese literature that combines universal human concerns and values with Chinese form.[103] Although his transformation cannot be solely attributed to visiting the IWP, he has advocated that Chinese writers "understand the West thoroughly but write independently to attract their attention," echoing the late-Qing scholar Wei Yuan 魏源, who promoted the idea that China should "learn advanced technologies from the West in order to vanquish the West" (*Shi yi changji yi zhi yi* 师夷长技以制夷).[104] More importantly, the perhaps surprising "popular turn" of contemporary Chinese writer-instructors points to the shifting ecosystem of literary production and reception in China, which, as will be illustrated in the following chapters, has been characterized by tightening ideological control from the party-state on the one hand and deepening commercialization in an increasingly consumption-driven economy on the other.

3

THE UNEASY WRITER

In this chapter, I look at both the theoretical and creative output of contemporary Chinese writers to contextualize their entry into institutions of higher education as founders, administrators, and faculty members of creative writing programs, which I will then examine in depth in the next chapter. Chinese writers' formal installation at Chinese universities not only strengthens existing networks but also builds up an ecosystem that seeks to bring together those who produce and those who study literary works and then harness the synergy of this alliance. Their literary production and theoretical discussions following and surrounding that momentous happening envision a virtuous cycle of literary production, consumption, and critique, and they show the utopian potential of literary production. Along with their reflections on the roles of writers and literature in contemporary Chinese society, their creative endeavors not only demonstrate how they pursue a crucial aspect of their identity as creators and guardians of Chinese literature in practice, but they also, as will be shown in the next chapter, provide models for their students and train a future generation of writers and gatekeepers. Furthermore, the reception of their works inside and outside academia also reveals the inner workings of a literary market under state patronage and surveillance, which keeps an even closer eye on "serious literature" than it does popular literature, and which shapes cultural production through both discipline and rewards, including the top literary prize awarded by the Chinese Writers' Association to the best Chinese novels every four years: the Mao Dun Literary Prize.

The volatile setting of a postpandemic, postsocialist China complicates the official call for patriotic contributions by cultural workers, as market forces contest but also collaborate with stringent state ideological control to shape cultural production. Most recently, this has been made obvious by writers' responses to the party-state's request to "tell good Chinese stories" (*jianghao Zhongguo gushi*

讲好中国故事). On October 16, 2022, at the twentieth CCP National Congress in Beijing, CCP General Secretary and Chinese President Xi Jinping 习近平 reported on the party's achievements during the previous five years and presented his vision for China over the next decade on behalf of the Central Committee.[1] Under Section Eight, titled "Building Cultural Confidence and Strength and Securing New Success in Developing Socialist Culture," he elaborated on his earlier emphasis on telling good Chinese stories.[2] He stated, "We will stay firmly rooted in Chinese culture. We will collect and refine the defining symbols and best elements of Chinese culture and showcase them to the world. We will accelerate the development of China's discourse and narrative systems, better tell China's stories, make China's voice heard, and present a China that is credible, appealing, and respectable." His proclamation to tell China's story better boils down to an attempt to represent a positive image of the nation to the outside world and to advance the nationalist agenda of projecting strength and extending Chinese cultural influence globally. It answers to domestic imperatives, too, since Xi promoted it to build the "cultural confidence" of the Chinese people and thereby to legitimize CCP rule and solidify his comprehensive control of national affairs.

Xi's promotion of "good Chinese stories" had started as early as 2013, shortly after he took the top office in China in 2012. He had spoken about this idea at a variety of high-profile conferences, such as the National Conference on Propaganda and Thought Work (*Quanguo xuanchuan sixiang gongzuo huiyi* 全国宣传思想工作会议) in 2013 and the Party's Nineteenth National Congress in 2017. However, on the august platform of the Twentieth Congress, he not only fleshed out what constitutes "good Chinese stories," highlighting Chinese "roots" and listing cultural "symbols, elements, and discourse and narrative systems"—in contrast to a brief mention of the same term to "increase national cultural soft power," which he used at the Nineteenth Congress—but he also explicitly linked it with "strengthen[ing] China's voice in international affairs so it is commensurate with our composite national strength and international status." This latest speech came at a fraught historical moment. The CCP had to deal with the havoc wreaked by a global pandemic, including some self-inflicted wounds, even though Xi would have wished for a victory lap: it was the first keynote speech he delivered at the party's national congress since securing uncheckable power through a constitutional amendment in 2018, which abolished term limits to the Chinese presidency. His edict thus hints at the motivation for the CCP to further tighten ideological control in cultural spheres as it attempts to deal with a multitude of challenges from home and abroad. More to the point, this slogan affects the intellectuals, scholars, and writers living under the rule of the party-state and shapes the kind of work and discourse they produce.

As Xi's call to tell good Chinese stories takes on new meanings and new urgency, party organs, faculty members and students at institutions of higher education, and even the state-run Chinese Culture and Media Company have produced numerous articles to interpret, supplement, and amplify Xi's message. They all promote "traditional Chinese cultural treasures" and advocate for integrating them into the telling of modern stories. They also unequivocally state that "good Chinese stories" should establish "socialism with Chinese characteristics" as the only path for national rejuvenation (*fuxing* 复兴), and they likewise validate the legitimacy of the current regime. However, they concede that good Chinese narratives must consider the diverse traditions and aesthetic preferences of international audiences and adapt effective foreign strategies to strengthen and spread the Chinese voice. Specifically, to tell Chinese stories better, writers must look for common topics, emotional resonance, and shared interests with international audiences while also deploying clear, vivid, and authentic language to deliver officially sanctioned messages. To achieve this goal, they further argue, Chinese higher education must produce "global talents" (*guojihua rencai* 国际化人才) who possess solid specialized knowledge, fluent English, media savvy, global perspective, and patriotic spirit, echoing some of the learning goals promoted by creative writing programs at Chinese universities (see the introduction).[3]

That the Chinese state would summon up its cultural workers to contribute to nation building is, of course, nothing new or surprising. In fact, throughout history, some Chinese scholars and intellectuals have willingly devoted themselves to the project of national salvation even at the expense of personal interests. But contemporary Chinese writers and intellectuals inhabit a different ecology than their predecessors, and as a result, they produce distinct types of works and embark on different career trajectories, such as teaching creative writing at universities. Below, I first present a short survey of modern developments of the Chinese cultural ecosystem to show both the continuity and shift of this venerable lineage facing contemporary writers. In the next three sections, I then illustrate, respectively through theoretical writings and creative works, the ways that writers wrestle with a number of questions: Who are or who should be their intended audiences? What goals, if any, should they aim for through their creative works? And ultimately, how can they achieve or retrieve a position of moral authority and cultural efficacy while securing a stable livelihood in contemporary China? I provide a detailed textual analysis of two novels authored by Sun Ganlu and Wang Anyi because as the most recent "cultural phenomenon," they can shed light on the dynamics of the contemporary Chinese literary market while also demonstrating how two representative authors pursue their writerly identity through literary content and form.

Elite and Popular Literature in Modern China

At three critical junctures in twentieth- and twenty-first-century Chinese history, the boundary between elite and popular literature has been renegotiated: the May Fourth New Cultural Movement in early twentieth-century China, the rise of internet literature in the new millennium, and the birth of university-based creative writing programs over the last two decades or so.[4] The evolving dynamics between elite and popular literature reveal shifting views on the roles of the writer and literature in Chinese society while producers and consumers of literature grappled with cultural modernization and a changing "structure of feelings"— or, "a common set of perceptions and values shared by a particular generation and most clearly articulated in artistic forms and conventions"—as their nation and culture underwent unprecedented transformations.[5] Each iteration of elite or popular literature also indicates changes in the sociocultural landscape of modern China, with moral authority, cultural prestige, and national status at stake and the content and form of literature in flux. Therefore, a look back in history can illustrate some of the hidden roots and stakes involved in the birth of university-based creative writing programs in China.

The establishment of creative writing programs at Chinese institutions of higher education has come from a sense of urgency felt by the cultural elites, though the founders have simultaneously taken advantage of official cultural-political policies to counteract the shrinkage of the humanities at Chinese universities and in society at large. Most significantly, the sheer volume, market share, and social energy generated by internet literature posed grave challenges to traditional serious literature in print form. In response to a perceived crisis facing highbrow literature, the literary and political establishments—embodied by state-sanctioned organizations such as the Chinese Writers' Association, its local branches, and their affiliated literary journals—search for new venues to reach a wider audience and make connections with younger generations while attempting to assimilate web authors into the existing system and enfranchise web-based cultural products. As universities build writing programs and offer courses in a variety of genres, including web fiction, established authors also seek to integrate popular narrative forms and evoke populist sentiments into their works in a bid to gain more market share and remain culturally relevant in the face of prevailing socioeconomic and political headwinds.

Still, contemporary writers of serious literature must shoulder more than their fair share of the burden of Chinese history and tradition, especially in terms of their sense of obligation to contribute to nation building through cultural production. The distinction between elite and popular literature has always carried more significance and emotional weight beyond the purely economic or even cultural; it has often represented and continues to signal political and moral power in China. This tradition dates back to the Confucian idea of literature as a tool of moral instruction and governance, which emphasized its didactic function more than its intrinsic aesthetic value or any ideas of artistic independence. Similarly, in the early twentieth century, modern Chinese intellectuals occasionally promoted Western literary forms and genres to aid certain literary groups—such as the Creation Society (Chuangzao She 创造社) and their advocacy of "art for art's sake"—but more often to represent social reality in their effort to remedy social ills and revive Chinese culture. In other words, the literary and cultural revolution they endorsed and organized was intended to contribute to nation building, confirming yet again the traditional Confucian conception of literature as a tool of social engineering. As happens with any project that is redemptive in nature and transformational in objective, these intellectuals formulated a narrative of a diseased and hopeless Chinese tradition as the foundation to begin "the work of modernity."[6] Although the scope and depth of the iconoclasm of the radical May Fourth intellectuals were arguably unique in modern history in general, the literary modernization associated with May Fourth also embodies radical intellectuals' paradoxical practice of replicating the role of the Confucian scholar-official to invent a modern self.[7] They reaffirmed the Confucian emphasis on the cultivation of the mind as an integral part of the transformation of society.[8] Their proposed literary modernization demonstrates a Confucian heritage that assigns literature as the vessel of the Way and accentuates the power of literature in transforming people spiritually.

The project of nation building through literary and cultural modernization undertaken by modern intellectuals shifted after the May Fourth period, and it gradually subsumed individual autonomy under nationalist political engagement. Without a doubt, literature produced by the May Fourth intellectuals represents a profound sense of individual and national crisis, generated by China's repeated defeats by foreign powers since the 1840s and its consequent semicolonization. It was thus unsurprising that many radical intellectuals readily embraced the doctrines of "national defense literature" (guofang wenxue 国防文学) during the second Sino-Japanese War (1931–1945). From there, it was also a natural step for them to flee to the CCP-controlled area in Northwestern China and join forces to produce literature to solidify a "united front" against Japanese aggression. Mao Zedong specifically called on intellectuals to learn from folk artists to produce a new kind of popular literature—by the people and for the people—to advance the goal of national salvation, a move echoed by his would-be heir, Xi Jinping, seventy years later.[9] Zhao Shuli 赵树理 was praised as a model of the revolutionary "peasant writer" for creating stories such as "Little Erhei Gets Married" (Xiao Erhei jiehun 小二黑结婚) and "Meng Xiangying Stands Up" (Meng Xiangying fanshen 孟祥英翻身), in which he used literary forms and themes familiar to the peasantry to propagate new ideas of "free marriage" and women's liberation from domesticity to join the workforce. In contrast, Ding Ling, a female writer originally known for her portrayal of discontented female intellectuals adrift alone in the modern city during the May Fourth period, came under severe criticism for exposing women's unique plights and advocating for their independent interests in the purported revolutionary utopia of Yan'an 延安, the headquarters of the CCP-controlled area.

Since the founding of the PRC in 1949, official discourses in China have always emphasized the utilitarian function of literature, regarding it as a tool of civic education that should mobilize the people under the banner of socialist construction. During the 1950s and 1960s, it was virtually unheard of to view literature as entertainment in China, even though this may have been desired by readers. Rather, the state sponsored a kind of "popular" literature that followed Mao Zedong's edict on literary and artistic production and that appropriated folk forms to propagate the CCP's policy of the day instead of representing "bourgeois" desires for romance and entertainment. Under such severe strictures, any description of a romantic relationship, not to mention sex, immediately made a literary work suspect in official eyes. As late as 1979, a short story titled "Ai shi buneng wangji de" 爱是不能忘记的 (Love Must Not Be Forgotten)—written by the female writer Zhang Jie 张洁 and today a canonized piece of post-Mao Scar Literature (shanghen wenxue 伤痕文学)— caused considerable controversy. Although the author portrays a self-sacrificing female protagonist who never acts on her secret love for a married communist cadre, this work roused criticism for allegedly espousing "bourgeois sentiments" just because it holds that individuals have a right to romantic love that is separate from the revolutionary cause and the ethical code of Communist China.[10]

A major paradigm shift in Chinese literary production came with the inception of Chinese internet literature at the start of the new millennium. Chinese web literature has come a long way from its beginnings. China is currently the world's largest broadband internet market.[11] As a site of dynamic cultural production, the Chinese web rivals printed channels. By 2000, web literature, consisting mainly of unedited items, had surpassed the volume of print matter published in China.[12] As literary production and consumption turned from didacticism to entertainment, authors and readers of web-based literature also shifted their gaze from the master narrative of nation building to more personal concerns and individualistic pursuits. Whereas radical intellectuals in the early twentieth century sought to establish their bona fides as architects of modern China through literary production, authors and readers of web-based popular literature in the twenty-first century unabashedly tout its distance from, and even rejection of, serious literature produced by cultural elites.

Chinese web literature represents important shifts in sociocultural life in twenty-first-century China: the rise of consumerism, the legitimization of cultural production for entertainment, and the decline of time-honored prestige conferred upon (male) intellectuals and the elite literature they produce, which was formerly recognized as the primary source of knowledge and authority. Yet it cannot help being shaped by various political, economic, and sociocultural forces. The state has tightened its already stringent control of web literature even more in recent years through multilayered censorship mechanisms ranging from authorial self-censorship, reader reporting, and monitoring by web administrators to surveillance and crackdowns by designated bureaucratic units at both the local and national levels. At the same time, web publishing and the franchising of popular works, including their adaptations into films or TV dramas and the sale of associated merchandise, have proved highly profitable thanks to enthusiastic fans and consumers.

Some of Perry Link's observations on romance consumption in early twentieth-century China could easily apply to web literature and its audience in the twenty-first century. Link characterizes the readership of twentieth-century popular romance works as middle class, and he argues their function was to provide comfort to overstimulated and insecure urban dwellers with rural origins who resented gaps between their expectations and their realities. He also highlights the role of new media (printed newspapers and picture books) in the spread of romance novels. But the internet, a different new medium, has generated several distinct features in Chinese literature as well. It provides a unique platform that enables Chinese users to express their opinions, likes, and dislikes at an unprecedented volume and with unprecedented candor and speed, despite the state's censorship attempts. Web literature is composed, published, distributed, and read differently than print literature. It generates innovative literary devices and blurs the boundaries between different genres, media, and ultimately, elite and popular literature. The web-based multimedia environment has shaped the form and content of web fiction. Web novels not only incorporate references to current events and web-induced lingo and writing styles, but they also utilize audiovisual elements such as music and images to complement and enhance the reading experience. Furthermore, new reading and writing practices have emerged, challenging the generic conventions of Chinese fiction. Serialized web fiction features narrative innovations such as *fanwai* 番外, supplementary chapters that present scenes from another character's point of view and provide an alternative narrative to the protagonist's account. New subgenres inspired by computer games, such as "[magic-]space" (*kongjian* 空间) fiction, or unusual gender benders, including matriarchal and homoerotic tales, have also appeared, potentially signaling social as well as literary changes and challenging the existing literary establishments and their affiliated cultural elites.

The participatory nature of online reading adds additional layers to the impact and significance of popular literature. Readers' discussions not only excavate and create meaning in the original web work, but they also help readers make sense of their own lives through their acts of extrapolation. They are, in short, engaged in creative play through which they express and manage the fears, desires, and fantasies that they otherwise lack the means and sense of security to explore fully and reveal to the (disapproving) general society. Web literature makes it possible for readers and authors to form what Matt Hills calls "a community of imagination," which constitutes itself "through a common affective engagement . . . and similar imaginative experiences."[13] Ultimately, the exchange surrounding these popular web texts, more so than the texts per se, reorients and recharges readers and authors with new relevancy and energy.

Nonetheless, the relationship between popular and elite literature is far more complex than it first appeared in the new millennium. Chinese web works reveal deep contradictions in their ethos, even as most of them have moved away from the grand official narrative of nation building. Ostensibly embracing playfulness and detachment and renouncing seriousness and meaning, Chinese internet literature cannot completely escape from processes of commodification and state surveillance, however. While women have become mainstay producers and consumers of web literature—apparently claiming cultural power from a male-dominated literary tradition—they still must contend with both gender-based discriminations in real life and misogynistic views expressed in web literature, sometimes even from their fellow female web users. Web users are not *always* resistant; *all* resistant readings are not necessarily progressive readings; and the "people" do not *always* recognize their conditions of alienation and subordination. Works of web literature sometimes also replicate state-sanctioned values and ideologies such as nationalist sentiments, xenophobia, and misogyny. As Stuart Hall notes, popular culture is neither "wholly corrupt [n]or wholly authentic" but rather "deeply contradictory," characterized by "the double movement of containment and resistance, which is always inevitably inside it."[14] Meanwhile, writers of traditional serious literature also strive for ways to tap into the energy produced by popular literature and popular culture in their efforts to find a path forward.

Theories and Debates

How do Chinese authors and intellectuals respond to the serious challenge from market-oriented and market-dominating web literature? Faced with the structuralist and poststructuralists notion of "the death of the author," how do they even begin to gain legitimacy while navigating Western theoretical quagmires, though Western theories were initially—and continue to be—hailed by some as welcome inspiration and reinforcement? Do their theoretical maneuvers mask acute anxiety about their identities as college professors, writers, intellectuals, and members of the Chinese middle class? Or do these represent strategies for self-advancement as they fight for title, tenure, status, recognition, and state funding at Chinese universities? An analysis of selected theoretical outputs and debates on creative writing can yield some clues to these questions.

Diao Keli of RUC, one of the foremost specialists of "author studies" in China, proposes a path to produce good Chinese writers amid the fierce competition for limited resources within and without Chinese academia. He paints his ideal author as a "thinker" well versed in both Chinese and Western literature who also has a deep understanding of all aspects of Chinese social life encompassing law, society, and the relationship between literature and society. To achieve that ideal, in his opinion, creative writing programs should not only teach writing skills but also provide readerly and theoretical training. He favors a dynamic approach to author studies, privileging research on the creative process and its distinct "author ecology" (zuozhe shengtai xue 作者生态学). Specifically, Diao emphasizes the importance of harnessing the synergy between author and reader in the internet age of "popular writing, everyone writing" (dazhong xiezuo 大众写作). In his opinion, since one party is easily affected and shaped by the other, a process of symbiotic mutual feedback should be cultivated between the author and the reader.[15]

Diao's theoretical construction concerning the making of an author and the creative process has been endorsed and echoed by intellectuals associated with Chinese writing programs elsewhere. The most distilled examples can be found in a series of interviews conducted by Shao Yanjun, a professor of Chinese literature at PKU, who was first introduced in the introduction. As PKU's MFA in creative writing program was dissolved by official edict, its former director, Cao Wenxuan, conceived of the idea of converting the program into the Institute for the Teaching and Learning of Literature at PKU. Cao proposed this entity for their now defunct creative writing program to sidestep bureaucratic prescription and maintain a semiofficial status. Although possessing its own budget, office, and staffing, the institute must yield its decisions on hirings and course offerings to PKU's Chinese Literature Department. In May 2021, the institute was officially launched, with Cao and Shao as its director and deputy director, respectively. Literary scholar and PKU professor emeritus Xie Mian 谢冕 (at age ninety) and Nobel laureate Mo Yan were retained as "consultants." They have also hired Li Er 李洱, the former deputy director of the Chinese Writers' Association's Modern Chinese Literature Museum and the recipient of a prestigious Mao Dun Literary Prize, as a tenured professor of creative writing. Supported by this stellar lineup, they announced that their goals consisted of educating and making two kinds of talents: for creative writing and for teaching Chinese literature at K–12 schools. They proposed to "hire famous authors to teach, invite authors for residency, design a systematic curriculum in literary appreciation and creative writing, initiate scholarly discussions, organize lectures and talks, and establish literary awards" to explore effective ways to teach creative writing and reform the teaching of Chinese literature at K–12 schools. What was left unsaid, though, was whether the institute would be able to recruit graduate students to pursue an MFA in creative writing again, though this remains the hope of the two directors according to word through the grapevine.[16]

The institute has thus far utilized Li Er's connections to organize a series of weekly talks by famous contemporary authors, though some guest speakers are also alumni of PKU's MFA in creative writing program. From September to October 2021, Shao also conducted a series of interviews with authors, scholars, and editors to explore this central question: How is the author forged? (*Zuojia shi zenyang liancheng de* 作家是怎样炼成的). The question references the Chinese title of USSR author Nicolai Ostrovsky's famous novel, *Gangtie shi zenyang liancheng de* 钢铁是怎样炼成的, or, *How Steel was Forged*.[17] The twenty-two interviewees range from their thirties to their seventies in age, and they roughly span two generations, but they are all engaged with literature in significant ways. Most of them are author-instructors, scholars, or administrators of creative writing programs at prestigious institutions of higher education in China. Some work as editors of literary journals after graduating from creative writing programs. They also produce works in a variety of genres, including serious literary fiction (short stories and novels), genre fiction such as science fiction and web literature, and literary criticism and scholarly monographs. Thus, to a great extent, this is already a self-selected group that is serious about and devoted to creative writing in one way or another.

The four interview questions focus on the following areas: 1) Can writing programs at institutions of higher education produce authors? Can creative writing be taught at all? 2) What is the relationship between literary production and criticism or research? Must scholars or critics have creative writing experience? 3) What would be the ideal relationship between authors, editors, readers, scholars, and critics? 4) A discussion of the phenomenon of a major literary journal *Shouhuo* 收获 (Harvests)—which is known for its publication record of award-winning works in serious literature, including novellas and novels, since its inception— having developed an app and online presence to attract readers.

Unsurprisingly, all those interviewed believe that creative writing can be taught in a university setting, though they envision different learning outcomes for creative writing courses and vary from lukewarm to passionate in their endorsements. Some hold that creative writing classes teach not just writing skills, literary forms, and ways of expression but also ways of thinking: reasoning, innovation, critical thinking, the appreciation of humanistic values and the essence of "literature," assessment, and planning. They also believe that universities can offer a unique environment to encourage and stimulate creative talent; by inviting experienced writers to mentor the younger generation and provide an apprenticeship of sorts, writing programs can provide hands-on training and help to turn dormant instincts or life experiences into knowledge and artifacts.

However, the interviewees are not unanimously confident that writing programs can produce writers. Some successes have emerged in the decade and a half since the first MFA in creative writing was established in China, yet, as some facetiously put it, only eggs can be hatched, and no stones can be turned into chickens no matter how good the incubator is. In contrast, most of them credit creative writing classes for developing good readers and even scholars, and some express contentment with producing cultural workers who have enough writing skill to make a good living in different jobs, including computer game design. Others also credit writing classes for setting up clearly defined goals and time limits and thus functioning as an accountability mechanism that is useful for students who are being trained in the writing craft. One considers writing programs as a sort of democratic process that helps those with less natural talent to develop into better writers, while another opines that nowadays, too many literary critics and scholars and teachers of literature have no instinct for good literature whatsoever, and they must gain some perspective on the creative writing process so as not to completely lose touch with writers.

As for their vision of the ideal relationship between the writer and the external world, most of them say readers and writers should mutually inspire but not restrict one another, and that writers should avoid catering to readers exclusively. While some hold that web literature is too commercialized, others retort that the belief that producers of serious literature can somehow transcend societal expectations and restrictions is just an illusion. Speaking of *Harvests* launching an app and using an online platform to publish serious literary works, some applaud the effort to "make friends" with the public, while others remain skeptical about how successful this attempt can be because traditional serious literature in print has very different mechanisms of dissemination and intended audience than web literature does. While some dismiss this belief as overstating the gap between print and web literature, others do express doubt about whether *Harvests* can reach a younger and wider audience merely with the addition of an online platform.

Interviewees commented that all stakeholders in literary production in contemporary China, even if they are not necessarily teaching creative writing at universities, are invested in building up a culture that is friendly and conducive to the creative process. They expressed anxiety about the future of serious literature and their roles as producers and critics of such literature precisely by advocating for, and perhaps even by fantasizing about, a virtuous, mutually reinforcing cycle of authors, readers, editors, publishers, and scholars coming together to produce top-notch literature that can both appeal to the wide public and garner critical acclaim, literature that is both "sellable" to the masses and praiseworthy according to current elite literary standards. This is an ideal widely shared but not readily achievable among contemporary Chinese writers of serious literature. As it turns out, famous contemporary authors, some of whom also teach creative writing at high-profile institutions of higher education in China, have devised their own strategies to balance the popular and the elite and to combine accessible content with critically acclaimed craft in their works.

"The Last Avant-Garde"

Huang Ping 黄平, professor of modern Chinese literature and creative writing at East China Normal University (ECNU), remarked upon the release of his collection of short stories, *Songjiang yiwen Lu* 松江异闻录 (*Strange Tales from Songjiang*): "Nowadays literature is competing with *Douyin* 抖音 [the Chinese version of Tiktok]."[18] He therefore feels justified attracting younger readers by deploying popular themes and traditional storytelling techniques such as those lifted from premodern Chinese literature, including *Liao Zhai zhi yi* 聊斋志异 (*Strange Stories from a Chinese Studio*). In so doing, Huang and many of his peers are effectively emulating successful web authors in utilizing popular narrative forms to tap into Chinese readers' basic fantasies and desires.

In the case of Sun Ganlu, a contemporary author and Huang's colleague at ECNU, the adoption of popular narrative strategies appeared to be a drastic departure from his earlier works, and it sent shockwaves across the mainland Chinese literary world. Almost three decades elapsed between Sun's first novel, *Huxi* 呼吸 (*Breathing*), and his most recent, *Qianli jiangshan Tu* 千里江山图 (*The Painting of One Thousand Miles of Rivers and Mountains*). During those thirty years, he left his job as a mailman in Shanghai, joined the Chinese Communist Party, became the number two leader in the Shanghai Writers' Association, and eventually was appointed as a faculty member and the director of the Research Institute of Chinese Creative Writing at ECNU. The simplistic life sketch above, however, cannot capture the sharp U-turn that Sun has apparently taken with his newest literary creation. *A Thousand Miles of Rivers and Mountains* has readily gained state approval and endorsement. It garnered official accolades only six months after its publication in 2022, being recognized as a "tribute to the twentieth Party Congress" and winning a "Building Spiritual Civilization" award from the Chinese government. Most recently, in August 2023, it won a Mao Dun Literary Prize, along with four other works selected from all the Chinese novels published between 2019 and 2022. However, this work was also mourned by some scholars as an elegy to the Chinese Avant-Garde Movement of the 1980s and even as a kind of "sellout" to the market economy in contemporary China. Supporters praise its effective execution of a "red narrative" (*hongse xushi* 红色叙事), its intricate narrative structure, and its return to "native" storytelling traditions in using concise language and emphasizing action rather than interior, psychological depiction. Critics, on the other hand, remark on its apparent capitulation to conventions of "genre fiction," its lack of psychological depth in characterization, and especially the stark contrast between this novel and Sun's last one, *Breathing*, which to them embodied a paragon of avant-garde experimentation with language and narration.

To be sure, this novel differs from Sun's last novel in various startling ways. However, rather than obsessing on whether it marks the end of the Chinese avant-garde, I posit that we should view this work as a hybrid fictional experiment that combines both Chinese and Western literary devices and attempts to hit the sweet spot between elite/modernist and popular/genre fiction. While an omniscient narrator masterfully propels the plot forward along linear sequences in the time of the story, the novel as a whole, including several pieces grouped by the author at the end as "appendices," points toward far more complicated narrative time and subverts this teleological progression. Ultimately, this novel represents Sun's effort to carve out a viable space for modern Chinese writers caught between the powerful pull of the market and the equally if not more powerful control of the party-state.

The reception of this novel shows that Sun's effort to walk an ideological and artistic tightrope has been amply rewarded; it has gained scholarly attention and state recognition despite the controversy it created. Since its publication in 2022, Shanghai academics, together with representatives from national and local media, have organized several workshops to discuss this novel, and they have published a series of articles in state media and social media afterward. These semiacademic activities have helped spread the work's influence nationwide and contributed to its eventual success in winning a Mao Dun Literary Prize. Within Chinese literary circles, they also testify to Sun's connections and stature, both of which have been enhanced by his "plugging into" university-based creative writing programs. The work thus merits a detailed analysis to not only showcase Sun's virtuosity but also reveal the acrobatics he must perform to gain a secure position in the contemporary Chinese literary market.

Sun has titled his novel *Qianli jiangshan*—literally, "A Thousand Miles of Rivers and Mountains"—citing his fascination with a painting with the same title by Wang Ximeng 王希孟, an artist from the Northern Song 宋 dynasty (960–1127 CE). Sun remarks that many undercurrents exist behind the grand panoramic view depicted in the painting, which resonates with his way of interpreting and representing historical events throughout the novel. His role as a novelist, he states, lies precisely in excavating the details buried by the long river of history and laying bare for his reader long-hidden secrets unavailable in existing historiography.[19]

Indeed, he intends to portray history through little details from ordinary lives. Just as one character in the novel cites from a Russian literary work he is translating, "There are no miracles in nature or history. . . . Yet there are so many rich contents . . . and unexpected events in any massive historical transformations, including any revolutions, that ordinary people regard many of them as miraculous."[20] Sun has studied memoirs, archival documents, and historical maps to piece together a plausible storyline when writing the novel. In the process, he has presented himself as the omniscient, transhistorical force that unearths truth and restores history. This authorial vantage point shapes the plot arc, characterization, setting, and message of the novel.

In terms of its plot, the novel appears to follow the generic conventions of suspense or espionage novels, though it deftly deploys cinematic techniques as well. It starts with a secret meeting of eleven underground CCP members who come from various corners of the city to gather in a secluded room in a public library located in Shanghai's foreign concessions a few days before the Chinese New Year in 1933. The narrative gaze, like an assiduous cinematic camera, follows each one of the members' footsteps while surveying the landmarks of old Shanghai—its movie theatre, library, wet market, dock, etc.—that teem with urbanites, rickshaw pullers, the police force of foreign concessions, and the secret police of the GMD. The omniscient narrator also introduces a little backstory, such as each of the characters' jobs or their random thoughts of the moment. From the very start, the narration highlights the modern, urban feel of the setting. These characters work in modern lines of employment; there is a real estate agent, a bank teller, a librarian, a physician, a taxi chauffeur, an elementary school teacher, a writer, and a journalist. Their backgrounds highlight not only modern means of transportation, communication, and education but also the fluidity and uncertainty of modern life as they flow from various origin locations outside of Shanghai into the modern city. The meeting is interrupted by GMD police who are eager to make arrests before it can start, and CCP participants scatter into the crowd of shoppers at the wet market. A chase ensues, with one secret CCP member, who did not attend the meeting though he was a part of the foreign concession police, jumping out of the window of a nearby house to alert his comrades and losing his life in the process. Bloodshed is then followed by the macabre atmosphere of prison in Long Hua 龙华, a suburb of Shanghai that housed the GMD police bureau. Here, the arrested CCP members are interrogated and subjected to physical torture, electric shocks, and psychological pressures. They are soon released by the order of a GMD spymaster who hopes to follow their traces to capture "the big fish," a top CCP leader then in hiding in Shanghai. As the story unfolds, the reader is treated to an action-packed narrative replete with intrigues between CCP and GMD special agents, chases, struggles, murders, and interrogations. The location, though mostly set in Shanghai, also shifts to Nanjing 南京 and Guangzhou 广州, as both the CCP and GMD spies engage in a life-and-death struggle to discover moles among their own ranks, to outwit the enemy, and, on the CCP side, to successfully carry out a task with the code name "Qianli Jiangshan."

Interestingly, the protagonist, Chen Qianli 陈千里—if one can classify him as a protagonist in a work that privileges the portrayal of a group of interfacing and intertwining characters rather than focusing on one individual—is a Russian-trained CCP secret agent and special envoy with family roots in Shanghai. The book title can thus also be interpreted as the man with the name Qianli weaving together various strands of the narrative while pursuing his mission among the one thousand miles of rivers and mountains of China. The author bestows on the CCP agent who saves the day the capability to navigate the chaotic, complex political and geographical landscape of China in the 1930s with relative ease, and to overcome daunting challenges to accomplish his mission, while his comrades succumb to GMD interrogations and executions. Chen's supreme ability includes standard tricks of the trade that befit a top-notch spy, such as physical strength, martial arts skills, super-alertness, coolheaded calculation, an amazing memory, and analytical skills. But he also displays a kind of superhuman ruthlessness that allows him to compartmentalize his feelings for his brother and other comrades and his eagerness to avenge the death of his CCP lover. In contrast, the other characters, even those meant to be "good guys," demonstrate various human frailties, including inexperience, impulsiveness, and vanity, that eventually lead to their downfall. Chen alone discovers the GMD mole with the pseudonym Xi Shi 西施—a reference to the beautiful female spy sent by the king of the Yue 越 kingdom to sabotage the rule of the king of Wu 吴, Yue's sworn enemy in the Spring and Autumn period (770–476 BCE)—embedded in the CCP cell, precisely by capturing overlooked details of his manners and life history. Apparently, the GMD spy is vain enough to boast to his lover about his exploits and is unwilling to give up his addiction to a certain brand of cigarettes.

While machine-like efficiency and impulse control can be attributed to the harsh training Chen has undergone in a USSR spy school in Siberia, where the instructors emphasize ridding oneself of any "excess" action and emotion, the novel also depicts normal human desires for bonding as stumbling blocks to carrying out missions and as causes for failure.[21] The essential human relations that Confucianism privileges as the Five Cardinal Bonds (*Wuchang* 五常)—those between ruler-subject, father-son, older brother-younger brother, husband-wife, and friends—are frequently distorted, rendered into a sham, and eventually destroyed. For instance, the GMD spymaster Ye Qinian 叶启年 not only uses his public role as a college professor to recruit for Dangwu Diaocha Chu 党务调查处—the Central Investigation Section of the GMD Party responsible for espionage—leading patriotic students into that GMD den of iniquity, but he also has his only daughter killed because she leaked GMD secrets to the CCP. On the other hand, Chen Qianli also places CCP interests above family bonds, not sparing his younger brother's life for the sake of completing the mission he is charged with. There are several pairs of romantic relationships depicted in the novel, but they are mostly revealed to be vulnerabilities that doom a revolutionary or anti-revolutionary. Even when the two individuals involved in the relationship remain truthful and faithful to each other, their relationship is frequently cut short by death. Without a doubt, friendships suffer the gravest casualty in a world full of deceit, betrayal, and camouflage. As Lingwen 凌汶, a female writer and CCP member whose husband has died for the revolutionary cause, remarks, "This struggle has been so cruel that many people have completely changed in the process."[22] Long periods of separation, the need for secrecy in espionage work, and frequent disruptions to communications by arrests and deaths all muddy the waters and leave the survivor in limbo, grasping about the fate of their beloved. As for the ruler-subject relationship, the novel spares no space portraying the greed, infighting, and power grab among different factions of the GMD, exposing the "enemy's" dysfunction and hypocrisy. Yet even among CCP members who have shaken off temporary hesitation and confusion, their devotion to the revolution remains inadequately explained and incompletely justified. The reader is left wondering whether youthful passion and righteous indignation can sustain the revolutionaries faced with the deaths of friends and family members and their intimate experience with torture and threats to their own lives, had they survived this special mission.

As relentless ideological struggles between the CCP and GMD rupture the social fabric, the setting of Shanghai also seems to present death traps rather than safe havens for CCP members. The diversity and anonymity of urban life, rather than proving advantageous for carrying out secret missions, instead rouse GMD suspicions and expose CCP agents. As one arrested CCP member muses after their secret meeting has been cut short by GMD police: "Who would believe that all those people from different lines of work who normally would not have crossed paths would gather just to gamble in a secret room, especially when they have so little money on them?"[23] Indeed, urban living may even detract from, or at least distract from, revolutionary devotion. The author has one GMD interrogator advise a young female CCP member that she "dress up prettily, go see a movie, and do some window shopping" instead of getting involved in dangerous CCP activities.[24] Furthermore, the narrative mostly presents group portraits by moving from one character to the next rather than focusing solely on one central consciousness. Daily experiences of ordinary people are rarely acknowledged, let alone enjoyed or celebrated, as the narrator predominantly trains his gaze on actors engaged in the lethal strife between the CCP and GMD. We do not see portrayals of ordinary citizens going about their daily routines unless they can function as a background against which the revolutionary heroes prove their mettle, or as family relations to the sacrificing heroes who can testify to the pathos and heroism of their actions. On more than one occasion, a joyous family or group meal turns deadly when police rush in to make arrests, when spies use it to spread disinformation, or when CCP and GMD agents vie to outwit the other through trickery and falsehoods.[25]

Judging by the geographical movements of the characters, the novel may even be interpreted as a tale of fleeing the big city. After all, it takes a special agent trained in the Siberian wilderness to come into the city to save the day. As most CCP agents in the city fall, Chen Qianli carries out the mission of One Thousand Miles of Rivers and Mountains to transfer a CCP leader originally based in Shanghai to the CCP-controlled "red zone," Ruijin 瑞金 in Jiangxi 江西province, which is located in China's agrarian hinterland. This echoes and reinforces the CCP-sanctioned historiography: when GMD destruction of CCP underground organizations derailed the CCP's original plan to subvert GMD rule in big cities, the CCP leadership modified their strategy and focused on developing their control in rural China instead. Thus, the little details of urban life the author claims he favors in this work appear to have lost ground to grand official historiography; rather than acknowledging the dignity and happiness of ordinary living in the city, the novel focuses on the end goal of escaping the dangers of the corruptive modern city for the morally superior and politically correct countryside.

To support the master narrative of the heroic CCP fight against GMD rule and explain why the CCP members willingly shed blood and sacrifice lives for the political and ideological struggles between the two parties, the novel includes comments from a "third-party" (*disan dang* 第三党) commentator, Old Meng (Meng Lao 孟老). He punctures holes in Ye Qinian's myth of the CCP leading his daughter astray and exposes his hunger for power as the real culprit.[26] Yet the CCP hero Chen Qianli remains the epitome of faith, resolve, and selfless devotion to the CCP cause. The author even has Chen confronting Ye in front of the tomb of Ye's daughter and Chen's dead lover, aiming to set up a contrast between good and evil and between authenticity and hypocrisy. But the novel does not completely fulfill the standard generic expectations of the "red narrative" advocated by the CCP or those of male-centered web novels espousing the aesthetic of *shuang wen* 爽文 (or, narratives that gratify readers' desires for validation and power). In contrast to "red classics" such as *Yehuo chunfeng dou gucheng* 野火春风斗古城 (*Wild Fire and Spring Wind in an Old City*), this work exposes the innate cruelty and denial of life entailed in ideological struggles rather than being an unambiguous validation of acts of heroism. Additionally, compared with the hero in a typical male-oriented web fantasy, Chen Qianli possesses the power of action, though he does not possess the former's overwhelming charisma and flawless winning record.

More importantly, the author also silences Chen, the only survivor of the deadly mission of 1933, and takes over the task of speaking for him and the CCP victims of that mission. At the end of the novel, Sun includes three extra pieces outside the plot of the novel: an anonymous letter by one CCP "martyr" executed at Long Hua, addressing a beloved; an excerpted oral history purportedly by a provincial museum investigator who interviewed Chen Qianli in the 1970s; and a list of CCP martyrs executed for their involvement in the mission. Just like the story presented in the novel itself, these pieces are fictional, though they are intended to achieve verisimilitude and add to the historical gravity of the novel. Unlike the story, the anonymous letter uses lyrical language to express the letter writer's romantic feelings for the addressee and their ideals for a bright future in the "new world." Seen against the list of martyrs, this letter can highlight the heroic mettle of CCP revolutionaries. But paired with the silent, enigmatic figure of Chen Qianli that is portrayed in the excerpted oral history, it also contains irony, or even satire. The author shows restraint when delineating the psyches of his characters, touching upon their thoughts and emotions only sparingly in the main story. Moreover, in the "appendices," he shows that when the new world finally arrives, the revolutionary who survived the bitter life-and-death struggle loses his voice and must rely on the author's literary maneuvers to preserve and pass on the passion, love, and devotion of those who have died willingly for the CCP cause. Thus, the novel proves more complex than its successful "red narrative" appears. Although it extols the heroism and self-sacrifice of CCP members, it also subtly undermines the flow of "positive energy" (*zheng nengliang* 正能量) promoted by Xi Jinping and embraced by many CCP members, subverting its revolutionary message. The assured hand that painted one thousand miles of rivers and mountains and the unwavering authoritative voice, however understated and restrained, ultimately belong to none other than the author himself.

One Thousand Miles of Rivers and Mountains does not lack ambiguity and contradictions in characterization and plot, of course. Yet those elements enhance the suspense of the novel rather than completely overthrowing the completeness of its narrative structure or challenging the authority of the narrator or the author. It thus sets up a sharp contrast with Sun's avant-garde novel, *Breathing*, which uses poetic language, focuses on psychological depictions, and frequently destabilizes its narration. Sun had turned to archival research as he prepared to write this historical novel, and he also invoked his experience of working as a mail deliverer in Shanghai to integrate geographical knowledge into the plot. In the novel, he references historical and literary figures such as Lu Xun, Feng Xuefeng冯雪峰, Qu Qiaobai 瞿秋白, Ding Ling, and even the German playwright Bertolt Brecht, who visited China in the 1930s. He also depicts historical landmarks such cinemas, markets, and foreign concessions in Shanghai, and he has even reportedly calculated the tidal waves of Wusong 吴淞Port near Shanghai—all in an effort to provide historically accurate details. Yet his skillful narration, characterized by his intricate plot structure and his deft appropriation of devices from both genre fiction and cinema, belies his modest self-representation as a "beginner" and "new learner" in this new line of literary pursuit. While some scholars applaud his "zero narration," one devoid of excessive emotions, as a return to native storytelling traditions, it can also be viewed as a nod to the style of modern Western writers such as Ernest Hemingway.[27]

Does Sun's newest literary experiment, with its tight narrative structure and careful exercise of narrative control, symbolize or override the postsocialist incredulity toward metanarrative? On the one hand, it does attempt to address and even remedy a loss of faith in socialism "as a social and political metatheory with a coherent present and a certain future" by restoring the status and reputation of "red narrative," in contrast to the parody and satire of the revolutionary narrative represented in the "new historical" novels of the 1990s.[28] On the other, the author asserts his role as a self-assured storyteller who can fulfill the important mission of uncovering historical truth, and he thus utilizes a positivist approach to establish personal credit. Seen in this light, this novel represents another experimental way to "address bewildering overlaps of modes of production, social systems, and symbolic orders, all of which lay claim to a fledgling world of life" in postsocialist China.[29] Sun's recent self-conscious literary experimentation is apparently on its way to achieve market success, as a TV adaptation of this plot-driven novel—to be produced by Tencent Video and two other companies—is already underway. More importantly, his remarkable transformation provides a perfect case in point of how the writer interacts with both the state and market through literary production in postsocialist China, and it can shed light on other contemporary Chinese authors who seem to be making a similar popular turn lately.

An Ode to the Ordinary

The Knife and Words (*Yi ba dao, qian ge zi* 一把刀，千个字), the most recent novel by Wang Anyi, who is also a faculty member and instructor of creative writing at a prestigious university like Sun Ganlu, has not enjoyed the same degree of success as Sun's work in terms of state recognition, even though it has also generated much scholarly interest and media attention and is not lacking in either craft or plot. Its lackluster official reception was perhaps partly due to the familiarity of its setup. After all, since the 1990s, Wang Anyi has been continuously producing stories in which old Shanghai features prominently, despite her rebuttal of Chen Yingzhen's "mischaracterization" of her as being only interested in writing nostalgic tales of Shanghai (see chapter 2). *The Song of Endless Sorrow* (*Changhen ge* 长恨歌, 1996), *Heavenly Fragrance* (*Tian xiang* 天香, 2012), and the most recent *The Knife and Words* (2021), are set variously from the late Ming dynasty (1368–1644 CE) to twenty-first-century Shanghai. But more "problematic" to the official eye, one suspects, was the kind of message her work delivers. In contrast to Sun's extolling of a CCP hero, Wang insists on representing what researchers characterize as a unique aesthetic of everyday life through her depiction of urban living. Wang has repeatedly refused to "dramatize" history—even traumas like the Holocaust or Hiroshima—choosing in this work to focus instead on how a "weedlike life crosses its own river in a mundane world."[30] Shunning the well-structured, tight-knit plot arc characteristic of Sun's work, Wang also privileges fluidity and ambiguity in narration.

While Sun uses Shanghai as a background against which significant historical events unfold in the bloody struggles between the CCP and GMD, Wang continuously focuses on minute details of everyday living in the city. *The Knife and Words*, her fifteenth novel, spans several locations in China in addition to Shanghai—such as Gaoyou 高邮and Yangzhou 扬州in Jiangsu 江苏province, and Harbin 哈尔滨 and other locations in Northeast China—and even features several sites in the United States: Flushing in New York City, San Francisco, Atlantic City, and so forth. Explaining the title she has chosen for the novel, Wang states that "the knife" references a chef's knife, alluding to one of the three typical occupations Yangzhou "migrants" to Shanghai used to take up, working as cooks (the other two typical occupations were barber and pedicurist in a public bath). "The words," which in Chinese literally means "one thousand characters" (*qian ge zi* 千个字), alludes to a line from a poem by the Qing dynasty gourmet-scholar Yuan Mei 袁枚. It describes the scene of moonlight shining on a bamboo grove in the famous Ge Garden (Ge Yuan 个园) in Yangzhou; the shadows of bamboo leaves cast by the moonlight make a shape like the character for "singular" (*ge* 个). Wang intends for this title to hint at the limits of language to convey meaning. "When the knife swoops down," she comments, somewhat elliptically, "it creates not sparks but words. And the author can show you only the bamboo, but not the images that moonlight has cast through the bamboo."[31] Thus, the knife and words of the title not only invoke the geographical location of Yangzhou, referencing the protagonist's hometown and the origin of his culinary skills, which he learned from Yangzhou cuisine, but they also set up a contrast between the material and spiritual, between craft and art, between the real and metaphorical, and even between the ordinary and sublime. But Wang also deploys her massive repertoire of literary skills to dissolve the potential conflict and tension represented in the dichotomy set up in the title. The novel realizes an aesthetic of the ordinary through its structure, narrative perspective, and language, integrating the extraordinary into the ordinary and celebrating the ordinary over the legendary.

The novel starts and ends with two global metropolises, New York City in the United States and Shanghai in China. Part I of the novel, comprising six chapters, loosely follows the center of consciousness of the protagonist, Chen Cheng 陈诚. It starts at a dinner table in Flushing in the 1990s. Chen, a Chinese chef renowned for private catering at New York City homes, wows the guests with not only the exquisite Yangzhou dishes he has created but also with the folklore and stories passed on from his teacher, a famous chef of the Yangzhou (Huaiyang 淮扬) culinary style. When the dinner party ends, he leaves, passes the terminal of the number seven train, and goes home. From the point that Chen arrives home, the narrative first flashes back to describe his experience growing up at the age of seven in a little alley in Shanghai in the 1960s and then moves to his experience in New York City, Gaoyou, and other locations. It does not follow a strict chronological order but rather jumps back and forth between the 1960s and 1990s, presenting an almost stream-of-consciousness-like flow. In the process, the narrative introduces various people involved in Chen's life: his father, older sister, aunt, neighbors, childhood friend, boss, wife, and so on. Far from listing a haphazard array of characters, the author delineates intimate interactions between Chen and the others through acts of daily living: shopping, eating, taking a bath, sleeping, and quarreling. The reader notices that his mother remains conspicuously absent. The Shanghai aunt who brought him up has carefully removed a family photo from the album; his older sister gets into a fight with a friend from the Shanghai alley for some puzzling, offensive words about prison the other has uttered; and he seems to have lost a part of an early childhood memory that was related to his mother.

The second part of the novel, from chapter 7 to chapter 11, gradually reveals the backstory of his parents, his older sister, and his mother's acquaintances in Northeast China and the US. The reader learns that his mother was imprisoned and executed for alleged political crimes against the CCP in the 1960s or 1970s, though she was later recognized officially as a heroic martyr, and her reputation fully restored, after the Cultural Revolution. Her life and death cast a long shadow, though, as her husband, children, and former classmates and colleagues all struggle with the trauma of her death and their own survivor's guilt even while trying to pick up the pieces of their lives in the aftermath and at times benefitting from government restitution for her death. In the last part of the novel titled "Afterwards" (houlai 后来), ostensibly a postscript to the novel, Chen, his older sister, and his father have all immigrated to the United States. In the last scene, Chen visits Shanghai again for his aunt's funeral, and he stands in front of the ruins of a former steel plant where he used to visit as a child, crying silently with all his might.

The tone of the novel is far more optimistic than this dark ending may imply, though. Chen perhaps mourns the death of his before-life in Shanghai and the decline of a blue-collar career, as many of the benefits and the associated pride of working a manufacturing job in Shanghai have disappeared amid China's turn to a market economy and globalization. Yet he has established a successful business in New York City, resolved marital issues with a wife who also stands for a mother figure in his life, and reconciled with his father and older sister over his mother's death. Furthermore, his return to Shanghai achieves closure in both geographical and spiritual senses. His earliest memory starts in Shanghai, and he pays his last respects to his loving aunt to fulfill his filial duties in the end. She acted as another mother figure in his childhood, making up for his biological mother's absence. In reciprocity, he demonstrates his Chinese cultural heritage by participating in her funeral ceremony, though he is already a naturalized US citizen.

Perhaps most significantly, the novel progresses according to a logic of change and fluidity rather than according to fixed locations and rootedness. Wang asserts that the inspiration for this novel came from both her experience in a summer camp in Shanghai in the 1980s and her residency in New York City in 2016. Fascinated by various business signs in Flushing that seemed to her to hide many secrets, she felt compelled to explore and create stories for this location. While delineating the previous and current life of a Yangzhou chef in Shanghai and New York City, the structure of the novel, she adds, does not follow "natural time" but rather the process of his physical and spiritual growth, while also reflecting the author's inner state at the time of writing.[32] Indeed, the message of change to survive and evolve sounds out throughout the novel. Most if not all of the characters' experiences testify to the old Chinese motto that "Trees die if moved but people thrive when they move" (*Shu nuo si, ren nuo huo* 树挪死, 人挪活). His aunt, older sister, and he all migrated to Shanghai from elsewhere in China. His father left his hometown in Yangzhou as a young man and relocated to Harbin. Eventually, all of Chen's immediate family settle down in the US. Moreover, Chen has honed his culinary craft by apprenticing under both an itinerant rural cook and a premier Yangzhou chef and by traveling and learning on the job in various parts of China.

To be sure, as a chef, Chen is frequently vexed by the inexplicable evolutions of Chinese-originated plants and animals in the US, resulting in completely different flavors of apparently the same ingredients.[33] While this description seems to reinforce the traditional Chinese view that local food specialties have to be raised in a unique geography and climate, it is counteracted by other commentaries about how changes would improve the quality of food items in the novel. The author has a Shanghai sent-down youth living in Northeast China voice the opinion that superb liquor originates from the meeting of rivers from the north and grains from south in Guizhou 贵州 province, and that "rice must be hybridized to thrive or face degeneration."[34] Even Chen's failure to secure an heirloom variety of eel (*ruan dou* 软兜), which purportedly can only grow well in rice paddies in southern China, is explained by the difference, not the inferiority, of geography and disposition of the "New World."[35] While the US boasts vast open land, South China's narrow waterways and crowded living breed a type of Chinese eel, "a depressed (*yinyu* 阴郁) species" that can survive in "the darkness of narrow ditches, stone cracks, and muddy caves, and on a diet of the lowest on the food chain."[36] Moreover, Chen has learned to adapt and make the best of what is available in the US. Even while disappointed by the lack of authentic traditional Chinese cuisine in New York City, Chen concedes this may be because "people cling to their childhood food preferences and our memories are kept on our tongues rather than in the brain," and that he is no exception.[37] He has subsequently pivoted to satisfy different clienteles and made a thriving business from his culinary skills in New York City. After all, both Shanghai and New York are cities of immigrants known as "melting pots" of different peoples, cuisines, and cultures. Chen has come across immigrants from mainland China, Taiwan, Hong Kong, Vietnam, Estonia, and many more nations during his years living in the US.

Change is not only manifested in the incidents and experiences happening at a location where the protagonist happens to reside at a certain moment, but it is also embodied by a constantly shifting narrative perspective. Already moving between different geographical and temporal frames, the narrative also mostly progresses from the bottom up and from the inside out. Although it starts in the neighborhood of the number seven subway line in New York City, the city is more often experienced from behind closed doors at home and in the store rather than presented in a panoramic view with broad, sweeping strokes. The narrative also moves with the senses, thoughts, and emotions of the center of consciousness that it occupies at any moment. Using lyrical language throughout the novel, and supplanting narration with strategically placed descriptions, the author slows down the velocity of the plot while emphasizing the emotional, experiential pull of the story. For example, as a young boy, Chen feels terrified and then fascinated by the loud noises, large crowds, and organized chaos in the steel plant and its affiliated public bath.[38] He is in turn attracted to and awed by large bodies of water in Gaoyou and Harbin and feels the mystical allure of nature.[39] Even Chen's mother, a revolutionary-minded young woman from Northeast China who is used to open spaces with sparse populations, experiences an epiphany when she is confronted with the densely populated and minutely plotted-out urban life in Yangzhou. She feels moved by "the crowded, petty, and ordinary details that merge into a harmonious whole," and she is surprised by "nature's meticulous planning and compassion for the human world" such living embodies.[40] This sentiment echoes Chen's ode to the seemingly unlivable environment that nonetheless breeds tasty Chinese eels, and it provides a perfect testimony to Wang's aesthetic of the ordinary life.[41] Just like the eel that can live on so little, Chinese urban dwellers make full use of very limited resources. Both have survived hardships to produce something beautiful and meaningful eventually.

As Wang states, the plot structure follows an interior, psychological logic rather than an external, temporal one. The narrative perspective similarly privileges internal rather than external action. Together with a lyrical prose that tones down action and accentuates description, it's no small wonder that Wang deftly turns the extraordinary into the ordinary in the novel. The story of Chen's mother could easily be rendered into a heroic or tragic tale. However, seen from the perspectives of her spouse, children, and colleagues, the novel, on the one hand, sheds light on her character as an ordinary human being with her own share of youthful indiscretions, limitations, and human failings. On the other, it emphasizes not just her legacy and impact on ordinary lives but also the dignity and meaning of ordinary lives per se, precisely by delineating how those ordinary lives manage to interpret, integrate, and eventually make sense of both her death and their own experiences, intertwined as they are. Ultimately, the message seems to be that not everyone can achieve acts of extraordinary courage and selflessness, yet it is perfectly acceptable to embrace our limits and pursue our happiness, however mundane it is compared with the life and death of a revolutionary hero.

Wang Anyi validates rather than critiques ordinary living, reinforcing her love for the ordinary by laying bare the daily minutia that is often complicated by subtle human psyches and interpersonal interactions. "Big Shanghai" (Da Shanghai 大上海) may be an oxymoron, since residents only "see a slice of the sky from narrow alleys, with the sun and moon hanging on a corner of the buildings."[42] But it is precisely the kind of dense, close-knit, and repetitive day-to-day living that bestows meaning and provides an anchor to otherwise unremarkable existences. As Wang states, Chen Cheng eventually arrives at a kind of "moral life" that is "simple, pleasant, comfortable, and free from sufferings," almost on a par with what the protagonist in Leo Tolstoy's novel *Resurrection* has accomplished through atonement.[43] *The Knife and Words*, in affirming and privileging ordinary day-to-day living more than dramatic acts of heroism, thus also addresses "the fundamental predicament of modernity"—"How to affirm the value and dignity of ordinary life without abandoning a sense of the heroic, without giving up the quest for a higher life?"—in its unique way.[44] Therefore, even though this work has not won the same prestigious awards or had the same financial success as Sun's novel has, Wang enacts a form of "lateral politics" through her persistent pursuit of an aesthetic of the ordinary, refusing to be pulled in by the grand narrative of China's rise or be "worn out" by countless "red narratives" of the CCP's bitter struggles and eventual ascent to claim national power.[45]

Conclusion

Sun Ganlu was not the first avant-garde author to have made a popular turn in contemporary China. In fact, he credits Ma Yuan 马原, another big name in the

Chinese avant-garde literary movement of the 1980s, with pointing him toward a new way of storytelling. Following Ma's advice, he made the decision not to "overtask his reader" anymore with the kind of cryptic, poetic language he used in *Breathing*.[46] Sun attributes the style of the earlier novel to a specific life stage full of confusion and anxiety when he hit thirty in 1989, though one suspects the Tian'an Men Incident on June 4, 1989, marking the end of the "honeymoon period" between Chinese writers and artists and the party-state, also played a major role. Furthermore, Ge Fei, another famous Chinese writer who teaches creative writing and chairs Tsinghua University's Center for Literary Creation and Studies in Beijing, has long turned away from avant-garde literary pursuits to producing more accessible novels. He has by all accounts done well in his career. Other than publishing multiple award-winning works such as his "Jiangnan Trilogy"—*Renmian taohua* 人面桃花 (*Beauty and Peach Blossom*), *Shanhe ru meng* 山河入梦 (*Mountains and Rivers Come to Dreams*), and *Chun jin Jiangnan* 春尽江南 (*Spring Ends in Jiangnan*), which came out between 2004 and 2019 and earned him a Mao Dun Literary Prize—he is now a tenured professor at one of the most prestigious institutions in China (with "Chinese MIT" as its moniker), vice chair of the Chinese Writers' Association, and the recipient of a "a special subsidy" awarded by the Chinese State Council (Guowu Yuan 国务院) to recognize high-achieving cultural figures.

However, the Jiangnan Trilogy met with harsh criticism from Can Xue, a female Chinese author consistently producing avant-garde literary works, who has, incidentally, been more widely studied, translated, and anthologized abroad than most contemporary Chinese authors. To her, Ge's works, and those of most other contemporary Chinese authors who advocate a return to the native and traditional, just demonstrate an "inferiority complex." She opines they were too cowardly and lazy to study foreign works deeply and instead took refuge in denying the commonality of human experiences and uniform standards to judge the quality of literature. In contrast, she insists that good literature must delve into the deepest human subconscious, and she criticizes the "flatness" or the lack of any psychological depth or "spiritual dimension" in most Chinese novels.[47] Can Xue's low opinion of contemporary Chinese literature and her peers sets up an interesting contrast with Huang Ping's position, which holds that "readability" alone can endear a literary work to younger generations and lure them to the world of serious literature. For him, the literary techniques learned from genre fiction combined with deep "literary value" would be the ideal middle ground. "Fiction needs to be read first," he insists. But what exactly is "literary value"? On this point, he is less clear, only stating that literature should not be just about "*shuang*," and it should not simply satisfy the basic readerly desires for power without considerations of inner logic.

Contemporary Chinese writers' literary experiments, their sometimes startling reversals of their earlier style, and the contradictory receptions they encounter, reveal the shifting politico-cultural landscape of postsocialist China. But the Chinese avant-garde of the 1980s had never been a univocal movement of resistance to begin with. Researchers show that a reputedly "open" Chinese government at the time in effect bribed experimental writers to stay away from politics in exchange for government financial and policy support.[48] In the 1990s, moreover, a type of "package dissent" emerged, as "artists had gradually learned how to combine political acuity and market sense to produce works that earned them enough notoriety to advance their careers but not so much that they were banned."[49] As shown in this chapter, contemporary Chinese authors must each explore their own way of being in the world through artistic creation. Market pull, state control, and institutional and other local factors can produce different literary configurations and different career paths. One of the most viable options and perhaps also one of the last sanctuaries, as it has turned out, is Chinese academia.

4

THE (NOT-SO-) RELUCTANT TEACHER

Mark McGurl sees "the true originality" of postwar American literature in "its patron institutions." By turning "writers into salaried writing professors and students into tuition-paying apprentices," he claims, the graduate writing program makes creative writing as American as apple pie.[1] The Chinese story, however, demonstrates a somewhat bifurcated path to cementing the relationship between the writer and the school. Talented and ambitious young writers in China face similar challenges—confronted with the hard choice between a devotion to their art and a paying job—to their counterparts in the US, and only some of them are fortunate enough to secure a stable faculty position to teach writing in Chinese academia. However, Chinese universities also take the initiative to recruit famous writers to join their faculty as consultant, part-time adjunct, or full-time long-term faculty members, in effect creating a two-tiered system of faculty appointments in their writing programs. Both types of writing faculty members contribute to the development of the writing program. But the latter group claims more of the limelight, not just because of their higher profile as established authors but also because their presence on campus represents a new, if not entirely unprecedented, shift in Chinese higher education—having published writers teach creative writing. This phenomenon can partly be attributed to its model, the American-style writing program represented by the IWW, but ultimately, it reveals the specific political, economic, and sociocultural conditions that have made such a radical change possible in postsocialist China.

Chinese universities such as PKU and Fudan often attempt to craft an origin story that traces the founding of their creative writing programs to a "glorious tradition" that saw famous writers of the early twentieth century teaching at their institutions. The boundary between creative endeavors and the systematic study of literature, or between the disciplines in the humanities and those in the sciences, may have been less starkly drawn than it was after the founding of the PRC in 1949 and the adjustment of colleges and departments in the 1950s. Yet this type of founding narrative, aiming to generate cultural capital, reveals a deep-seated anxiety provoked by uncertain ideological winds and the stiff competition between institutions for financial and human resources, rather than representing the truthful and gritty details involved in making a program. Thus, in this chapter, I pursue the intricate dynamics between individual, institutional, and state-level actors who have participated in building university-based Chinese writing programs from yet another perspective: writers as instructors in Chinese higher education. They have mostly revised the classic workshop-style of teaching that originated from and was disseminated by IWW, adapting it to address specific local needs even while they tout their American model.

Below, I first discuss the individual and institutional motivations for Chinese writers to teach Chinese-language creative writing in academia. I then present in some detail various approaches to teaching creative writing based on fieldwork and other research findings. While the focus of this chapter remains on mainland China, especially on Wang Anyi's example, I also bring in cases from Hong Kong and Taiwan. In Hong Kong, universities offered their first set of Chinese-language creative writing courses in the 1980s at the Chinese University of Hong Kong, though the first-ever Chinese creative writing course was offered as early as 1968, by IWP alumnus and Hong Kong poet Dai Tian 戴天.[2] Taiwan's institutions of higher education started to offer creative writing courses as early as the early 1960s.[3] The longer histories in teaching creative writing at these two sites yield critical insights into the unexpected fast growth of creative writing programs at Chinese universities over the last dozen years. Finally, I end with salient contrasts and comparisons of the experiences of writer-instructors in mainland China, Hong Kong, and Taiwan, such as their adaptations of the workshop model, their similar reliance on leadership support from home institutions, and their pragmatic concerns with graduates' employment prospects.

To Teach or Not to Teach

Having published writers teach creative writing represents a notable shift in Chinese higher education in the post-1949 era, despite claims about the "return to traditions" from some Chinese academics associated with various creative writing programs who are nostalgic about the past and eager to defend the legitimacy of their programmatic existence. Nevertheless, it has quickly become the norm for Chinese institutions of higher education ever since Fudan established China's first MFA in creative writing in 2009. Still, there are two types of writer-instructors at Chinese universities. They are recruited through and serve on separate tracks once they are hired, and they each contribute to the writing program from their specific habitat, even while collaborating to professionalize and Sinicize creative writing in the new millennium. Regular, full-time writing faculty are hired through the standard process governing the hiring of any other faculty. They are required to have a doctorate as a terminal degree at the application stage, and they are expected to teach a full or even above-average course load as early career faculty. They also undergo the same review process for tenure, promotion, and salary raises as faculty in other disciplines. Their strength and record in publishing creative works, though it may work to their advantage at the recruitment stage, may come back to haunt them as they become more integrated into Chinese academia. Most institutions do not consider publications in creative writing as legitimate faculty scholarship, though they do make exceptions for famous writers who have been specially hired to build their creative writing programs. Rather, they demand their early career faculty publish research and scholarship in high-ranked academic journals, especially those listed by the Chinese Social Science Citation Index (CSSCI), and they track citation numbers to calculate "impact factor" while remaining oblivious to the index's bias against disciplines that are not based on quantitative analysis. Young faculty members often struggle to produce sufficient "scholarship" while juggling a heavy teaching load, family responsibilities, and creative pursuits. The other type of writing faculty, in contrast, have established themselves as celebrities before entering Chinese academia. They are frequently middle-aged or older, they have had varying job experiences before becoming full-time writers, and they have published creative works at a high volume or been the recipients of national and international literary awards. Holding special appointments made by the universities, they do not go through a regular recruitment process, and they enjoy many benefits not available to their junior colleagues. While this chapter focuses on this group of writer-instructors, I stay mindful of the plight younger writing faculty members face, even as I seek to shed light on the complex dynamics and ramifications of the two-tiered faculty system at Chinese writing programs.

Given the increasingly volatile politico-economic milieu in postpandemic China—especially the challenges confronting writers such as how to make a living and how to maintain a traditional cultural heritage associated with the profession of authorship—it may not seem such a surprise for them to accept job offers willingly and even enthusiastically from prestigious Chinese universities. After all, a teaching position means a regular paycheck, which is more reliable than living on royalties, and increased job security is further complemented by the prestige associated with working as a college professor at a top-tier institution. They are, in the humorous albeit apt words of Shao Yanjun, pursuing *mingfen* 名分, or the proper position and title that Confucianism would deem befitting of the cultural elite.[4] For established writers, the attraction of a college faculty appointment also lies in the freedom and intellectual stimulation it ostensibly promises, which contrasts with what is available from the traditional state-sponsored mechanism that supports full-time writing.

For Yan Lianke, Wang Anyi, and other famous contemporary Chinese writers, the state provides financial support to make it possible to engage in full-time writing. The national Chinese Writers' Association (Zhongguo zuojia xiehui, or "Zuoxie" for short) and its provincial branches dole out a limited number of positions for full-time "professional writers" (*zhuanyue zuojia* 专业作家). They offer a salary and do not require regular in-office attendance, though these salaried writers are expected to participate in weekly or monthly "study sessions" together, which typically involve reading and discussing the most recent policy documents and edicts from top CCP leaders—usually President Xi Jinping—in the central government. Modeled on a similar system prevalent in the former USSR, Zuoxie has not only invested heavily in the collective indoctrination of its members, but it has also extended its reach beyond the immediate environs of major Chinese metropoles such as Beijing and Shanghai. Rural youths interested in cultural production and especially in creative writing used to be able to drastically change their life trajectory for the better by submitting creative works to prestigious state-run literary journals and by making a name for themselves through publication, if only often with generous editorial help. They would then be appointed as a cultural cadre and admitted to the local branch of Zuoxie or another state-sponsored cultural institution, and they would eventually leave their poverty-stricken hometown for a better life in the city. But since the 1990s, this has proven to be a path less accessible due to the decline of state-run literary journals and local cultural institutions. In recent years, Zuoxie has also started to hire independent contractors. Called "*qianyue zuojia* 签约作家"—or "contracted" instead of "professional" writers—these authors do not enjoy the same privileges as the other group, though they are expected to produce more creative works. For example, they may not be granted a secure household registration (*hukou* 户口) in Beijing or Shanghai, and they are thus unable to avail themselves of many social welfare assistances that would help them buy a car or a residence, or have their children enrolled in a good public school.

Such a state-run system for the "cultivation of writers," while apparently offering financial security and freeing up time for creative endeavors, comes with strings attached as well. At best, the state prescribes what is appropriate content and form for the writers on its payroll. At worst, its insidious influence leads to self-censorship and self-sabotage, even among the most talented writers. In contrast, a faculty appointment seems to offer the free inquiry of knowledge and the pursuit of creative inspiration among like-minded literary enthusiasts, if not experts. Yan Lianke, for one, extols the "freer and purer" environment afforded him by the creative writing program at RUC compared to his prior experiences in the military and as a member of Zuoxie. Compared to faculty in creative writing who are recruited through the normal channel—including younger writers who have successfully published creative works but are still required to earn a PhD before starting work and are expected to shoulder a heavy teaching load before they earn tenure (if applicable) or promotion—these specially appointed writer-instructors enjoy far more leeway when working in Chinese academia. A lighter teaching load, a generous salary, and adulation from young students represent some of the extra perks.

On the demand side of the equation, associates such as faculty, students, and alumni of Chinese writing programs all regard the union between established writers and writing programs to be a match made in heaven, not least because the integration of famous writers into Chinese academia provides another rationale for the existence and expansion of creative writing programs. Some compare established writers to car mechanics and drivers, and literary critics and traditional instructors of literary history and theories to designers and engineers, and they clearly view writers as more effective writing instructors than the other group because of their richer hands-on experiences in writing and publishing. However, they also consider it "ludicrous" to expect writing instructors to produce writers on their own. Not all writers are good teachers of writing for one thing. For another, even if it were possible to transfer writing experience from an instructor to a student through osmosis, which sounds unlikely, it still would not automatically produce good writers. The birth of a successful writer depends on many other factors, such as natural talent and opportunities. Society does not require a math professor to produce mathematicians through teaching college courses, they argue, so why ask the same of an instructor of writing?

Indeed, the apparently win-win arrangement between institutions and writers does not yield consistent results. As writers frequently struggle to adapt to the unique ecology of institutions of higher education, the effectiveness of writer-teachers' engagements in the Chinese academy remains a focus of public attention and even a source of tension. Wang Anyi teaches writing at Fudan, apparently to great acclaim from both her students and colleagues. However, student complaints have also arisen about superficial engagement or cool neglect by the writers, and about those writers' "unstable, unsustainable" teaching quality when it is compared to that of other faculty members at the home institutions. Some big names in contemporary Chinese literature are said to be able to give a couple of lectures but not independently teach a course, even though they have been hired into the faculty of creative writing.[5]

Thus, a deep scrutiny of how these writer-instructors teach in Chinese academia, examined from different perspectives, can cast light on the remarkable metamorphosis of authors into teachers and the ramifications of that process. As mentioned previously (see chapter 1), although specific course offerings may vary from one institution to the next, there is much overlap between the curricula of different Chinese writing programs. Their courses typically include required general education courses, major requirements in craft, elective courses aiming to develop students' aesthetic discernment, seminars for students to interact with guest speakers, and, finally, internship experiences. What calls for further investigation, of course, does not lie in what's on the books but rather what is involved in the writer-instructors' specific pedagogical practices. Chinese writing programs face a unique set of challenges compared to their US counterparts. They usually lack sufficient teaching staff to meet students' needs. Many times, a program administrator complains about the shortage of competent teachers for their courses, even and perhaps especially if a famous author accepts their offer. Faculty members hired through the normal channels are expected to carry heavy course loads and even overloads, with their creative writing courses discounted as part of their regular load at times. On the other hand, a published and established writer may not be as good a teacher of writing. Wang Anyi is recognized as a rare model of success. Respected for the innovation of her own work and her knowledge of the newest trends in literature at home and abroad, she seems to possess both the requisite theoretical base and the creative writing credentials. She has also proven to be an effective instructor in the classroom. Yet most specially appointed famous authors are only expected to give a few talks rather than teaching regular courses. At the most, they also serve as one of the two advisors for a student's thesis, working alongside a regular, full-time, on-campus faculty member who works as the student's academic advisor. The criteria for their promotion and salary raises also diverge from those experienced by regular faculty members.

Given the general lack of college-level teaching experience and even a lack of interest in teaching on the part of established authors, it would seem unrealistic to expect them to readily learn from and teach in the style of a foreign model such as the Iowa Writers' Workshop, regardless of what the program administrator has claimed as their inspiration. Furthermore, even enthusiastic adaptors of the Iowa model at Chinese universities do not fully embrace it. Some faculty members fault it for being too skills-oriented and lacking in theoretical grounding,[6] while others criticize it for being too obsessed with word choice or grammar and for missing the big picture when assessing students' work.[7] Additionally, Chinese visitors to UI derived pedagogical inspirations not just from the set mode of workshop teaching alone. To be sure, they praise the attention paid to subtle details in literary works at the writers' workshop in contrast to the kind of "general feedback" writing students typically receive back home. However, they are far more impressed with the general milieu of seriousness about literature and creative pursuits, the open exchanges about writerly and translational craft between visiting writers and workshop students, and the rich array of cocurricular activities, including ad hoc workshops on translation, authors' readings, theatre performances, and other interactions between book writers and book lovers in Iowa City.[8] Unfortunately, when Chinese visitors return home, they often see their US-inspired vision for program building collide with Chinese reality. Chu Yunxia, who spent a year at UI from 2015 to 2016, deeply immersed in IWP programming, recalls that she found her UI experience hard to replicate back home at BNU. She cites among major obstacles the lack of effective writing instructors (regardless of their successes as writers), which makes leading workshops to polish students' writing skills infeasible for sure. She also notes that Chinese students are typically too shy or too reserved to read their own works aloud in public, let alone to offer feedback or critique their classmates' works.

Under such adversarial circumstances, what effective Chinese writer-instructors have accomplished inside and outside the classroom constitutes a tale of faith, flexibility, and innovation. In what follows, I summarize the textual and fieldwork findings from various programs located in mainland China, Hong Kong, and Taiwan to demonstrate how instructors have adapted the workshop model, what roles individual writer-instructors have played, and what the implications of their executions have been for student learning. I focus on writing programs at Fudan, PKU, and RUC in mainland China; HKBU and HKUST in Hong Kong; and NKNU and NTHU in Taiwan, while also bringing in other programs—such as Tongji's low-residency model, and SHU's especially well-developed undergraduate and graduate programs and its outreach efforts—as appropriate.

The Shanghai Experience: Wang Anyi at Fudan

Often hailed as a role model not just by her students but also by fellow writers interested in teaching in the Chinese academy, Wang Anyi has in fact subverted the workshop structure to make it work in the Chinese context. To state it simply, she invokes her authority as an established writer to instruct students rather than duplicating the allegedly egalitarian workshop model in a wholesale manner. Much of her success as a teacher of writing comes from her clear, authoritative, and consistent instructional voice, even as she adopts some of the micro-techniques of workshopping creative works in the classroom.

At the core of every American-style creative writing program is the writing workshop, or the so-called "Iowa model" because it originated there. In its strictest form, it works like this: Classmates evaluate and write detailed comments about students' work, then sit around a table and "workshop" the piece. The writer sits silently while classmates comment first on what is working and then go back around to comment on what is not. The instructor weighs in. Only then can the author respond. With an instructor-leader facilitating peers' freely offered feedback, the Iowa model ideally would provide an egalitarian and sustainable structure that helps students grow into better writers. However, numerous scholars have noted not only its inherent contradictions but also the precarious status of the classic model in our postmodern, poststructuralist internet age.

For one thing, they point out the "rigidly hierarchical" spatial dynamics—one workshop leader sits before six to fourteen students—even as all voices are ostensibly given equal time and equal weight. For another, achieving workshop harmony can be a challenge as the classroom experience is often affected by "bitter jealousies, competition," and writing to please instructors and fellow students.[9] In our period of the frantic push for publication, when students publish work alongside their professors, some even argue that "the scourge of the workshop is not top-down indoctrination but a decidedly bottom-up antiauthoritarian malaise and arrogance." In addition to the students' "conflicted sense of centrality," the writers' workshop juxtaposes three spaces conventionally kept separate by working authors: "the compositional space, the performative space, and the critical-reflective space." Since the author is literally caught in the act of composing while being requested to perform the work as if it were complete, this leads to a "paradox of procedure." The audience, largely untrained critics, is in effect asked to aid with their classmate's authorial growth while remaining ignorant of the author's artistic aims. The Iowa model faces even more challenges that can be seen in the context of the typically short attention span in "our time of incredulity."[10] Given the monotony the workshop setup inflicted on participants who are all well-versed in the basic tenets of poststructuralism, it is surely unrealistic to expect from them earnest devotion to a work not yet fully formed (and that possibly never will be) day in, day out.

In contrast, Wang Anyi's writing pedagogy, partly a self-conscious rebellion against the Iowa model, has worked out remarkably well at Fudan. A 1983 alumna of the IWP, she visited classes at the famed IWW during her residency in Iowa City, specially arranged by Hua-ling Engle. She was underwhelmed by the workshop sessions, however. To her eye, class time was spent mostly on grammatical issues, and it became "boring" to sit through such technical nitpicking every day. It was not until the Sinophone writer Yan Geling introduced her former writing professor John Schultze to teach writing at Fudan during the 2007–2008 academic year that Wang Anyi's own writing pedagogy began to take shape.

Before Fudan launched its MFA in creative writing in 2009, Wang Anyi had suggested that they invite Yan Geling, who had academic credentials, a publishing record, and critical acclaim under her belt, to visit Fudan and teach. Yan in turn introduced Schultze. The creator of the Story Workshop Method of writing instruction, he had taught in the Fiction Writing Department of Columbia College Chicago for many years, training writers and teachers of elementary and secondary schools by using the Story Workshop techniques. Wang Anyi sat through all his classes at Fudan for four weeks, alongside some other faculty colleagues and students who were perhaps less diligent though equally enthusiastic to learn, including Yan Feng 严锋, currently professor of modern Chinese literature, and

Zhang Yiwei, now assistant professor of creative writing and then an MA student in literary writing at Fudan (more about her later). When the year was up, Wang Anyi went to her friend, Chen Sihe, a literary critic, modern Chinese literature scholar, and the chair of the Chinese Literature Department, and offered to teach in the same style going forward, confident that she had mastered the workshop techniques. Her course on fiction writing, a perennial favorite with the students, subsequently came into being.

Wang Anyi combines textual analysis of translated foreign classics and writing instruction when she teaches the craft of fiction writing, a signature course in Fudan's MFA program. She has led students through a series of reading, analysis, and critique of translations of world-famous works, including Victor Hugo's *Les Miserables*. She has subsequently published her lecture notes as stand-alone volumes, such as *Xiaoshuo ketang* 小说课堂 (*Fiction Classroom*). She also utilizes a modified and scaled-down workshop model to teach writing. For example, she has sometimes requested students each produce an opening of a short story to share and be critiqued in class, workshop-style. She has also required them to brainstorm and collectively write a short story together for practice. She has made pedagogical modifications at least partly to adapt to enrollment pressures, for she lacks the capacity to provide in-depth feedback to each individual student's full-length completed work. But she has remained a dedicated and serious teacher since the very beginning; back then, she prepared an individual teaching plan for each class meeting, wrote out lecture notes in long hand, and was always at the ready with index cards in class.

Not only does Wang Anyi take her teaching seriously, but she also demonstrates to her students through both her creative works and classroom instruction that writing is a serious pursuit regardless of one's future career choices. In all her writing classes, Wang always emphasizes the inner logic of the story. Giving students copious feedback in class, she frowns upon "lazy" authorial moves such as randomly creating new characters to move the story along or "killing off characters" if they prove to be too much of a drag on the plot. Her tireless creative efforts through the years—which have resulted in numerous acclaimed publications and reaped domestic and international literary awards, just like her classroom teaching—have also impressed upon her students the need for hard work and self-discipline as a working writer. However, Wang has no illusion that Fudan's writing program can make published and successful authors on its own. Regarding writing as an "elite" occupation only accessible to a select few, she believes creative writing programs can produce more "practical" talents for the state, as preferred by the Chinese Ministry of Education, generate revenue for the university, and help students find gainful employment once they are armed with a good diploma. Her role as a writing instructor, she states, is just to help students enjoy and understand literature better than before and to get a good diploma at the end. She prefers students with less prior writing and publishing experience before entering Fudan's writing program, though, since she considers published authors "too set in their ways" to be taught and to learn anything useful from her. But she is confident that Fudan's MFA in creative writing has a rigorous selection process that only admits the most qualified applicants. In contrast to "some programs" that admitted forty students the first year they opened, she claims Fudan at first only accepted twelve, a number even lower than their allowed quota of fifteen. Fudan required applicants to take the standard national entrance exam and then followed up with careful additional departmental vetting before admitting students. Wang Anyi also stated with pride that Fudan had the "best faculty" in Chinese literature teach their writing students and that applicants to their MFA program were graduates of colleges with higher and higher national rankings through the years.

Her students, in turn, have been deeply impressed with Wang's seriousness about literature, even while acknowledging that her criticism is sometimes hard to take. Fu Yuehui 甫跃辉, an editor at a renowned literary journal in Shanghai and a rising young writer in his own regard, mentioned that Wang criticized his writings "80 percent of the time" when he was a graduate student at Fudan from 2007 to 2010.[11] Yu Long Kit 余龙杰, who now teaches Chinese creative writing courses at HKBU but who was enrolled in Fudan's MFA in creative writing from 2013 to 2015, also recalls that Wang often questioned why he wrote in a certain way. Her probing not only prompted him to reflect on his writing more deeply at the time but also provided a model of teaching. Nowadays, he also asks his students the same question in class.[12] Perhaps more importantly, all the students also feel that since Wang is an "equal opportunity offender" who critiques everyone's writing, there is no favoritism involved, and they view Wang as a fair and rigorous teacher. Consequently, the rare praise from her would raise their spirits tremendously. In fact, some students would use a cell phone to record her praise in class and play it back repeatedly later, just so they could keep that feeling of elation a little longer to boost their morale. In our interviews, the students and alumni all painted her as a demanding teacher in class, pointing out shortcomings of students' writing relentlessly in front of the whole class, but they also respected her as both writer and teacher. To them, Wang Anyi's guidance could save them a lot of time and trouble in their pursuit to become a good writer. Left to their own devices, they would most likely have struggled futilely much longer.[13]

Of course, the halo effect of having famous authors as teachers of writing cannot be underestimated. Without a doubt, some students feel the draw of programs that enlist big names in contemporary Chinese literature, the same way fans flock to their idols in contemporary popular culture. Indeed, they take selfies with Wang Anyi in class, and they unanimously extol the "privilege" of interacting with her and learning from her writing experience. However, they also have a point that in the eye of the public as well as enrolled students, teachers of creative writing carry more authority if they have written and successfully published creative works themselves. Since Wang is affiliated with Fudan, a top-ranked institution of higher education in China, the halo effect of the program is further enhanced by the additional allure of a top-notch diploma, a must-have in the competitive Chinese job market and especially attractive to students who have received their BA from a second- or third-tier institution.

Additionally, Wang's other official role as the one-time chair of the Shanghai Writers' Association has also proven useful in both practical and academic terms. In 2008, Wang launched the Shanghai Writing Program (SWP). Modeled on the IWP, the SWP invites emerging (usually young and rising) international writers to apply and come to Shanghai for a two-month residency in September and October each year. It was through her stewardship that this program grew and remained strong for the last decade or so. Her leadership has not just developed Shanghai's reputation as a culturally vibrant city with soft power and good living, in practical terms, it has also provided a venue, if not a platform, for Fudan students to engage in the international literary scene. Time and again, Wang invited famous writers, artists, and performers to the Creative Writing Summit, a required advanced-level seminar at Fudan's MFA in creative writing. SWP writers in residence also visited Fudan again and again. In 2019, for the last SWP before the COVID pandemic and the only one in the last three years, the theme was "Imagine Community," echoing President Xi Jinping's promotion of "community of mankind that shares the same destiny" (*renlei mingyun gongtongti* 人类命运共同体), implicitly with China as its leader. That fall, the Shanghai Writers' Association shepherded a group of ten international writers from England, Egypt, Italy, Russia, Jamaica, Belgium, Brazil, and Thailand around town. The visiting writers also came to interact with the MFA in creative writing students at Fudan. In an open forum on September 17, 2019, they talked about their works and careers first and then took questions from the students.

In fact, students of writing programs are willing to pay good money for opportunities such as these: purported apprenticeships under renowned writers (ideally at a first-tier university) and in-person interactions with other famous contemporary cultural figures. At Fudan, the MFA in creative writing program has expanded from a two-year program for a set fee of RMB $70,000 in 2009 to a three-year program with a total bill of $100,000. Tongji charges $30,000 per year for a two-year program in creative writing, but it adopts a low-residency model that enrolls part-time students who have classes only on Saturday and Sundays. Do the students think it is worth their investment of time and resources? All of those I interviewed said yes. Not only do they offer the information that an MFA in writing is less expensive than some other professional degrees, such as those in publishing or finance, but they also have high praise for the good value of the program itself.[14] Confirmation bias aside—which could orient those committed to the program to unconsciously seek only affirmative evidence to rationalize their choice—the students' approbation of the rather stiff price tag also reflects the emergence of affluent Chinese middle-class parents who are willing to pay a premium for their children's education. Furthermore, my interviews of these students reveal several common threads underlying their positive views of the program. Above all, the students regard being taught by famous authors such as Wang Anyi to be a major draw of the program. Some of them are fans of her work and her writing style, while others have always been dazzled by her reputation. Still others have favored Fudan over institutions in Beijing because of the mystique and glamour associated with Fudan and Shanghai. Some disparagingly comment on the somber, "stuffy" Beijing universities and their privileging of "practical writings" or applied writing rather than pure literature. In contrast, in their eye, the Fudan program represents the last stronghold for serious academic and literary pursuits. It sits on a campus that seamlessly combines Chinese and Western architectural elements to create a feel of "low-key luxury" (*didiao de shehua* 低调的奢华) in a modern, Westernized city full of energy and vitality. Thus, the program, the institution, and the city all come together to create the perfect experience for these devotees of Fudan's MFA in creative writing.[15]

Writer-Instructors in Hong Kong and Taiwan

As can be expected, Wang Anyi's success as writer-instructor is more the exception than the norm among her peers and her generation of successful writers in China. Famous Chinese writers hired to teach writing courses are frequently not able to do well not only because they are not trained in writing pedagogy but also because of their full schedules and multiple engagements, including their mandatory political commitments, which are not, as a rule, unmitigated joys. Hong Kong has consequently emerged as an alternative space for established mainland writers to explore their passion for teaching and develop pedagogical skills. Yan Lianke is a perfect example. As the founding writer-in-residence at RUC's MA in creative writing (*chuangzao xing xiezuo*) program, beginning in 2013, he visits HKUST every year and stays for at least two months to give public talks and teach a few courses, such as "Twelve Lectures on Nineteenth-Century Writings" and "Twelve Lectures on Twentieth-Century Writings;" he has published a volume of lecture notes on each as well. In his courses, he aims to share writing methods and experiences by leading students to read and analyze translated classics in world literature. Each enrolled student is required to complete a short story by the end of the course as a graded assignment. Quite a few of his students have published short fiction and novels after they have taken his classes. He notes that HKUST students generally lack background knowledge in literature compared to their mainland peers, but they show great enthusiasm for creative writing, with some even wishing to switch from their STEM majors.

Yan has earned an endowed professorship as IAS Sin Wai Kin Professor of Chinese Culture at HKUST, with the help of Liu Jianmei 刘剑梅, a professor of Chinese literature who collaborated with her father, the famed Chinese literary theorist Liu Zaifu 刘再复, to establish creative writing courses and launch a lecture series that has featured some big names in contemporary Chinese literature, including Su Tong 苏童, Yu Hua, Chi Zijian, Zhang Wei 张炜, and the Nobel laureate Mo Yan. Liu Jianmei's initial goal was to add humanities course offerings on a heavily science-and-technology-oriented campus and enhance the intellectual community therein (*tigao wenhua fenwei* 提高文化氛围), very much following the model of her alma mater, PKU. It has proven to be heavy going for her as a lone workhorse among the faculty. With humanistic fields already marginalized at the institution, their supportive president is also set to step down soon, leaving the future of creative writing uncertain to say the least. Liu Jianmei reveals that she organized various events on her own time and that her program-building efforts would not count toward her scholarship or lead to salary raises or promotions. Her pursuit of a stable degree-granting program in creative writing at HKUST has been unsuccessful thus far, and the pandemic has exacerbated staffing shortages, as most mainland Chinese authors were too constrained by the government's zero-COVID policy to come to Hong Kong over the last two years. She has expressed envy for apparently well-established and well-endowed creative writing programs in mainland China and for Taiwan writers, who, according to her, "all have faculty appointments at universities." However, she still touts the value of HKUST's creative writing courses. She claims that their students continue to rate the creative writing courses as the "best classes they have taken at HKUST," and some have published creative works as a result of completing their courses. She also praises the lifelong impact of creative writing courses and claims that they build students' soft skills. However, when some students wanted to switch majors to the humanities, both Liu Jianmei and Yan Lianke regarded it as a bad career move that would upset their pragmatic parents, and they dissuaded the students from doing so.

Indeed, "practical" and "pragmatic" are some of the most common descriptors by creative writing instructors and program directors to characterize Hong Kong students and parents alike, even in the case of HKBU, whose creative courses and programs seem to have fared much better compared to HKUST. HKBU launched a BA program in bilingual creative and professional writing in 2012 and a one-year MA program in bilingual creative and professional writing in January 2023. James Shea, an American poet who earned an MFA in creative writing from the IWW, started to work there in 2014. He currently teaches poetry writing, among other courses, and serves as the director of HKBU's Creative and Professional Writing Program and as associate director for their International Writers' Workshop, which is modeled on UI's famed IWP. When asked how HKBU succeeded in establishing a creative writing program against the general decline of the humanities and Hong Kongers' famed pragmatic mindset, he reveals that they were able to offer a degree-granting program thanks to a fortuitous confluence of various factors: the state initiative to focus on "cultural and creative industry" in Hong Kong; an understanding former dean, Zhong Ling 钟玲, who holds a PhD in comparative literature from the University of Wisconsin-Madison, is a published novelist and has befriended many contemporary authors; and their ability to self-brand and market to the public effectively. While the Hong Kong government promotes innovation and creativity mainly for the utilitarian goal of developing its economy, this policy focus has allowed academics to seize the opportunity to expand and build on creative writing programs. Shea and his colleagues have branded their writing program as offering "creativity-inspiring undergraduate education," and they have obtained support from senior leadership to establish it at HKBU. They have also lobbied their dean to modify the criteria for tenure and promotion for creative writing faculty. They convinced the dean to count creative works as scholarship for the writing faculty and to allow the writing faculty to create their own list of journals as acceptable and respectable venues for publishing creative works. Moreover, they market their program as both creative and practical, since it promises to teach students both creative and professional writing and thus to quell the qualms of parents worried about their children finding a good job after graduation. The creative writing faculty members at HKBU also believe that with their strong staffing and rich experiences, they can meet the needs of an underserved niche market by offering a bilingual MA in creative writing specially designed to attract mainland college graduates who are interested in learning about the West but who do not have the requisite resources or who have parents worried about the potential conflict between China and the US. Moreover, in their mind, their program would integrate Hong Kong's colonial heritages, such as the British educational model—which typically has a one-year rather than multiple-year MA program—and local strengths in English learning with the new reality of life under CCP rule and prevailing control from the central government in Beijing. Given the controversy surrounding the establishment of a creative writing minor in English at City University of Hong Kong just a few years before, the move to offer courses in both Chinese and English and to train students in bilingual writing is not only pragmatic but also politically astute.

Of course, program building cannot succeed solely on meticulous planning and perfect design without effective pedagogical execution. Here, Shea's and other HKBU faculty members' prior training in and experience with Western-style writing programs come in handy. Although Shea identifies a few differences between teaching writing in the US and in Hong Kong, and in English versus in Chinese—such as the amount of reading assigned to the students and use of electronics in class, including smartphones and PowerPoint slides—he believes his writing pedagogy stays essentially the same as the Iowa model. After obtaining a seminar—rather than an auditorium-style—classroom and cutting down enrollments to under twenty-five students per course, both of which took some effort on his part although they were eventually successful, he now has students sit in a circle and teaches in the workshop style. He claims that viewing students more as "practicing artists" rather than "students" or disciples helps to make his classes more engaging, the students more adventurous, and his teaching more effective. Thinking of everyone as a practicing writer, he "reads for art" rather than "hammering on grammar" when providing feedback, in sharp contrast to what students typically experience in secondary education in Hong Kong.

However, Shea emphasizes innovation in his teaching as well, even while paying tribute to the IWW. He states his goal is to help everyone "create new knowledge" rather than "reproduce old knowledge." He not only shows enthusiasm for students' works but has also developed creative ways to teach poetry writing, on which he has published several scholarly articles and book chapters. His methods include incorporating modes of translation as generative writing methods—such as homophonic translation, machine translation, and the translation of radicals of Chinese characters—into his poetry writing classes.[16] Acknowledging that Hong Kong students tend to be shyer and quieter than their American peers, he takes time to warm them up, calls on them more if needed, and organizes "silent workshop days," when students comment on each other's work in writing without speaking in public. He apparently prefers the "old-school" method of printing out hard copies for students to write their comments, hoping to help students focus and absorb more of the work under critique through a "tactile" experience. Yet he also uses a hybrid approach, combining the instruction of literary analysis and that of creative writing. He leads students to read English-language literary works and guides them to learn to appreciate and then emulate the literary devices in the original works in their own creative processes. He also notes with pride that their program has a "theoretical dimension," as the faculty integrates "creative writing with creative theory."[17]

Indeed, while they are faced with pressure from the market, the general shrinkage of the humanities, and increasing political oppression, the writer-instructors of Chinese-language creative writing based in Hong Kong—whether they are emigres from mainland China or Hong Kong natives—have all come up with innovative self-branding and pedagogies to eke out programmatic survival and individual actualization while helping their students move forward as well. In

Shea's scholarship on teaching Chinese-language creative writing in Hong Kong, he shows that for writer-instructors born and raised in Hong Kong, creative writing courses have also made it possible to foster self-expression and craft social critique among the students at Lingnan University (Lingnan), the Chinese University of Hong Kong (CUHK), and Education University of Hong Kong (EdUHK). The three writer-instructors that Shea has interviewed—Hon Lai-chu (CUHK), Mary Wong (Lingnan), and Wong Leung-wo (EdUHK)—all express a strong desire to help students "free themselves" now that residents seem to be losing freedom every day since Hong Kong's handover to mainland China in 1997. The specific pedagogies vary among the three interviewees, and they certainly differ from the Iowa model. They do not all use the workshop style to teach, they do not all emphasize revision or even provide written comments on students' writings, and they do not offer genre-specific writing courses. However, they all embed tacit social criticism by offering writing courses as a reprieve for students enmeshed in Hong Kong's traditional education system and oppressed by political pressure as well. In some cases, the rise of Cantonese in students' creative works also signals a desire and move to defend local Hong Kong identity and autonomy against increasing control from mainland China.[18]

Chris Tong (Tong Yui 唐睿), one of Shea's colleagues in HKBU's creative writing program, demonstrates yet another approach to teaching creative writing in Hong Kong. His parents immigrated to Hong Kong from Yunnan, China, in the 1970s, when he was about five years old. Initially resisting English-language instruction and literature as a marginalized "mainlander" at Hong Kong schools during his childhood, he directed his passion for literature and art to earning his second BA and MA in comparative literature from Université de la Sorbonne Nouvelle (Paris III) from 2006 to 2009. In 2009, he made another turn to study comparative literature and modern Chinese literature under Fudan's esteemed Professor Chen Sihe for his PhD degree. Nowadays, he not only teaches creative writing at HKBU as a published and award-winning novelist, but he has also established close ties with K–12 schools and literary journals and publishing houses in Hong Kong. Utilizing his undergraduate background in and passion about education, he has secured funding from Hong Kong's well-heeled Horse Racing Society to launch a series of outreach efforts and to integrate elementary and middle school students into the creative writing process. For instance, he coordinates with local theatres to provide immersive experiences for interested students, leading them to play different roles in a mystery, to try to solve the crime, and then to write and reflect on their experiences. The students' writings have been published and made available to the public, a testimony to the impact of the HKBU writing program for sure, though it more importantly is a record of innovative and public-facing teaching on the part of individual faculty members in Hong Kong.[19] Tong's friends and colleagues who are engaged in and employed by literary journals in Hong Kong also explain that they are working with the current economic-political structure, using funds from both Beijing and local charitable foundations to produce and disseminate literary works despite stringent ideological controls from both mainland China and Taiwan; unfortunately, after the passing of the national security law in Hong Kong in 2021, it is increasingly difficult to publish and sell their literary journals and works in Taiwan as well.[20]

In contrast to the more local-centered approach of native-born Hong Kong instructors, those who have spent formative years in mainland China tend to teach creative writing under the large umbrella of Chinese literature as world literature. It appears they have yet to learn the minoritized mindset or fully embrace the identity of local Hong Kongers. Yet different generations of writers with mainland Chinese roots also hold different views on the relationship between Chinese literature and world literature. Ge Liang 葛亮, the award-winning novelist and an associate professor in HKBU's Chinese Literature Department, also teaches Chinese creative writing courses for their writing program. Born into a scholarly family in Nanjing, China, in the 1970s, he completed his undergraduate education at Nanjing University (NJU) and then earned a PhD from the University of Hong Kong in Chinese literature. He had always envisioned for himself a career in research and academia, and he only started writing fiction when he was attending graduate school in Hong Kong. Winning the prestigious Taiwan Associated Literature Prize (Taiwan Lianhe Wenxue Dajiang 台湾联合文学大奖) motivated him to continue pursuing creative writing, if only in his spare time as a full-time academic. Ge notes that tenure and promotion reviews in his field of Chinese literature still only consider scholarly output, even though he sees the mutually beneficial synergy between his research and writing. For him, research can help him collect raw materials in preparation for writing fiction, while creative writing adds another dimension to his scholarly work, enriching the latter with emotional warmth (*wendu* 温度). Ge takes much pride in his scholarly work, remarking that for someone who finished college in mainland China, pursuing a graduate degree in Hong Kong really opened his eyes to the academic rigor and the amount of independent research a PhD program typically expects. However, he also takes his creative writing courses seriously. While expressing "envy" for the fast institutionalization of creative writing in mainland China, and while noting that all his creative writing courses are "elective" rather than "required" courses in his department, he has a clear vision for the learning goals and pedagogy of his writing courses. He does not believe that writing courses alone can produce writers. He instead aims to help students discover and develop their creative potentials and learn how to "dance in shackles"—that is, to master the rules of literature to excel. In his courses, he typically starts with reading literature, using literary analysis to demonstrate different aspects of creative writing, echoing a standard practice at both HKBU and institutions located in mainland China. Organized by topics, the course focuses on opening, ending, plot design, perspective, and character development in fictional works sequentially. Ge hopes to show the diversity and endless possibilities of literature in class even though he recognizes that a writer should establish a unique and consistent personal style. His students are asked to turn in three pieces of creative writing each semester to be graded, typically scaffolded from easier to more challenging tasks.

Combining literary analysis with writing instruction seems to be a common approach among Chinese writer-instructors in Hong Kong, including Yan Lianke, who is twenty years Ge's senior. But Ge does not seem as concerned with how Chinese literature can step into the world as Yan. "To successfully tell a good Chinese story to the world" represents an important edict issued by top Chinese leadership to the nation's cultural workers in recent years (see chapter 3). The two mainland Chinese authors who have become writing instructors at Hong Kong universities respond to this national cultural imperative in different ways, partially reflecting generational differences. Yan Lianke states that Chinese writers have the advantage of diverse and complex source materials, a rich native language, and rich literary traditions, while he decries the state censorship system that crushes creativity. He wishes for Chinese writers to take full advantage of their traditions and backgrounds while also engaging with universal humanistic concerns and the full complexity of humanity in their works. Only in so doing can they speak to broader audiences both abroad and at home even while ostensibly only telling a "Chinese story" through documenting Chinese people's current state of existence, he opines. Ge sees it as a given that a Chinese writer would always tell a "Chinese story," since "its origin and texture are rooted in the Chinese soil." Ge holds that the anxiety for Chinese literature to "step into the world" arose from and reacted to the apparent rise of Latin American literature in the 1980s, when García Márquez won the Nobel Prize in Literature. Ge believes those hoping for Chinese literature "to step into the world" already presume that a boundary exists between Chinese and world literature, while in fact, Chinese literature is and should always be a part of world literature. In this regard, he believes that creative writing programs have the potential to break down barriers by establishing a powerful channel for literary and cultural exchanges as instructors lead their students to learn from the treasures of world literature to guide their creative pursuits.

Of all three East Asian sites, college-level creative writing instruction has the longest history in Taiwan, dating back at least sixty years. Compared to the restless faculty members of young and "upstart" writing programs in mainland China, and struggling faculty at "middle-aged" writing programs in Hong Kong, Taiwan academics seem to have long embraced creative writing as part of their curriculum. However, they also acknowledge similar issues facing the humanities fields and have revised the classic pedagogy of teaching creative writing that originated at the IWW. At NKNU, faculty members in the English Department utilize creative writing as a tool for teaching second-language acquisition in the classroom, helping students to write stage plays and perform them using English. Similarly, those in their Chinese Department have integrated theatre and performance into creative writing courses; students write scripts for the local Taiwan theatre *gezai xi* 歌仔戏 while interacting with TV screenwriters and lyricists who are invited to visit their classes.[21] At NTHU, creative writing instructors have integrated analyzing literary classics, teaching the writerly craft, critiquing students' works one-on-one, and having students make oral presentations of their writings, implementing pedagogical practices similar to those adopted by their mainland and Hong Kong counterparts.

Interestingly, Western instructors of English-language creative writing courses have also noted "a deep-seated practicality" that goes together with the emphasis on "fact and memorization" among students in Taiwan, pointing out challenges facing Taiwan writing instructors like those experienced by colleagues in Hong Kong and mainland China.[22] Professor Lo Shih-lung 罗什龙, the former director of NTHU's Writing Center, which was founded in 2011 and was the first of its kind in Taiwan, remarks that MFA programs are rare at public universities in Taiwan, and they are concentrated mainly in institutions that specialize in the fine arts, such as Taipei Fine Arts University and the private Chinese Culture University. At NTHU, a national public institution that favors the study of science and technology rather than the humanities, their writing center initially offered First-Year Chinese Literature as a required credit-bearing general education course for all their students, along with English Writing Clinic, which can be credit-bearing or non-credit-bearing and is mainly designed to check English grammar. Since First-Year Chinese Literature originally focused on the study of Chinese classical literature, it proved unpopular with the students. It could not be canceled, however, since the faculty members teaching it were all established and tenured. The writing center consequently pivoted and offered three different kinds of courses on the appreciation of (classical) literature, creative writing, and academic writing. Writing courses then further bifurcated. Academic Writing has since remained a required general education course for all first-year students. Creative writing courses, on the other hand, are divided by genres into nonfiction, the essay, genre fiction, etc. and offered as electives for Chinese majors who take those in small classes, with an enrollment cap of about fifteen students. Academic Writing is taught in Chinese at NTHU to disgruntled STEM majors who claim they read and write mostly in English. The writing faculty countered this assertation by characterizing and publicizing their writing courses as an effective tool to train students in logic and reasoning, which are essential for all scientific research. In private, Lo argues that Taiwan is still a Chinese-speaking society and that students should not be trained in English only.

Yet faculty members in Taiwan also view their teaching as contributing to students' mental health. Lo praises the healing powers of creative writing courses. To him, a lot of the STEM students have serious mental health issues despite their excellent grades. They also have difficulty with long, sustained writing due to the negative impact of the internet and new media, which has inculcated an overreliance on smartphones and social media. Therefore, creative writing courses, more than training professional writers, offer a kind of "life education" (*shengming jiaoyu* 生命教育) by teaching students how to express feelings; they thus help students have a conversation with themselves and care for themselves. Lo admires the lyrical world that premodern literati-scholars purportedly inhabited, and he strongly promotes the efficacy of creative writing courses in teaching students how to "handle themselves." He even calls it "the use of uselessness" (*wu yong zhi yong* 无用之用), in the style of the Daoist philosopher Zhangzi 庄子, and an antidote to the prevailing Taiwanese mentality that narrowly focuses on employment prospects and the utilitarian function of education. The emphasis on the therapeutic value of creative writing courses seems to be a consistent theme in Taiwan academia, revealing a closer proximity to the American model in terms of learning outcomes compared to institutions in Hong Kong and mainland China, thanks to Taiwan intellectuals' longer engagements with the American-style creative writing programs and the influence of the IWW's Taiwan alumni, such as Bai Xianyong and Yu Guangzhong. The impact of this more student-centered and individualized pedagogical approach can also be seen and felt in mainland Chinese writer-instructors who have been educated in Taiwan, such as Zhang Yiwei at Fudan, who expressed similar views on the "utility" of creative writing courses as "emotional and life education" in our interview.

Professional Development for Writer-Instructors

Despite distinct state and local governmental initiatives, the curricular designs and pedagogical practices of writing programs at all three sites show some overlap. They all teach students the basic principles of writing, offer courses that guide students in appreciating and analyzing "masterpieces" of world literature, lead them to practice writing in different genres and critiquing each other's works, and, finally, require them to present their own creative works to the public. The professional development of writing faculty also remains a consistent theme. According to Diao Keli, a professor at RUC and a self-identified "witness" to the Sinicization of creative writing since 2010, there are two types of professors in Chinese writing programs: traditional literature professors who teach history, criticism, and theory, and established writers hired as creative writing professors. He calls on both groups to develop skills and become better integrated into the writing program. He holds that the former use traditional pedagogies to disseminate the knowledge of literature, history, and philosophy, but they do not know much about the creative writing process. In contrast, the latter can share their experiences as writers but need time to think deeply about the rules of creative writing and the meaning of literature. He would like for professional writers to explore what "literature" really means, reflect on writing techniques, and innovate by finding new ways of writing and creating new materials. He looks to the literature faculty to identify the strengths and weaknesses of the American model, adapt it to Chinese needs, and offer fewer courses in theory and more that train students in writing skills.

The writing programs discussed in this chapter, however, reveal that the younger generation of writer-instructors have already combined writing experience with theoretical training. More importantly, the success of a writing faculty member or that of a creative writing program in mainland China, Hong Kong, and Taiwan does not lie so much in the writer-instructors' self-improving individual endeavors as it does in the overall support structure they may or may not find at an institution and at the national or societal level. Many a program administrator cites national and local governmental policies and initiatives that have made it possible to professionalize and programmatize creative writing at their institution. In this regard, success in recruiting famous writers as full-time or adjunct professors does benefit the formalization and institutionalization of creative writing. The regular faculty and administrators of writing programs often work with these "celebrities" to lobby government officials for resources, space, and general policy support to develop their programs. Presumably, the famous writers more readily have the ear of higher-ups—thanks to their higher profile and wider influence in society—than ordinary academics do, and they also bring with them established networks of writers, editors, and publishers.

As mentioned previously, HKBU has taken advantage of the Hong Kong government's emphasis on "creative and cultural industry" to launch their bilingual writing program, while Fudan has seized upon the Chinese Ministry of Education's policy focus on educating more "practical talents"—or competent workers rather than academics—to start the first MFA in creative writing in China. Additionally, Yan Lianke, one of the cofounders of RUC's writing program, worked with his colleagues to convince the Chinese Ministry of Education to allow their writing faculty to design their own set of entrance exams rather than using standard national exams in English and political thought. They were able to have more flexible criteria for educational background, admitting students with a bachelor's degree or its equivalent. RUC is thus able to enroll talented writers who are frequently turned away by other programs due to their low grades in the mandatory English or political thought exams or their lack of a college diploma.

Furthermore, whether they are located in mainland China, Hong Kong, or Taiwan, the thriving of a writer-instructor and a writing program frequently depends on a supportive senior administrator, be it a dean, president, or even an especially well-connected and powerful department chair. Residing in an institution of higher education, writing faculty and programs must also meet expectations of institutional citizenship, such as contributing to a general education curriculum, generating revenue, attracting and recruiting students, pacifying paying parents, and raising the domestic and international profiles of their program. While these extraneous responsibilities may not necessarily detract from faculty teaching and creative efforts, they can distract faculty who are already burdened with a heavy workload from realizing their full potential as writers and teachers.

In-group dynamics also matter. Wang Anyi, for instance, has the luxury of calling most of the shots when running Fudan's creative writing program. This is not just because she is a highly respected author and teacher of writing on her own but also because she has been given free rein from the very start. With the support of the department chair and senior leadership at Fudan, she has most, if not all, of the decision-making power in staffing, student recruitment, and curricular design. It is murmured that she handpicked the current codirector of Fudan's MFA in creative writing, and most faculty in that program were former students of hers. Wang has undoubtedly devoted much energy and effort to building up Fudan's program, but the ability to mold the program according to her own vision must have also generated immense motivation and satisfaction.

Yan Lianke also reveals that RUC's writing faculty initially approached Mo Yan for the position of writer-in-residence, but they quickly realized he had too much on his plate in terms of public demands and publicity engagements after he won the Nobel Prize in Literature in 2012. Yan Lianke, on the other hand, was inspired by Wang Anyi's success at Fudan and was happy to oblige. He feels that RUC's writing program has utilized the two-tiered faculty system to its great advantage: younger members of the program with traditional academic training teach a variety of courses in history, theory, literature, or writing in different genres, while established writers like him or Mo Yan can give public talks and engage with individual students as advisors and mentors. Of course, their creative writing curriculum has enjoyed more leeway than their peers from the very start. Helped by a more flexible admission policy, enrolled MA students in creative writing also have only one required course at RUC: Political Thought. Their faculty and students can therefore devote more energy and space to discussing and practicing the writerly craft. Yan believes this kind of stimulating environment provides "fertile soil" for the growth of writing talents while also remaining a source of great joy for the teaching faculty. In this regard, Yan Lianke's vision and rationale for RUC's writing program may prove an outlier compared to its peers in mainland China, Hong Kong, and Taiwan, one more on a par with the American model. Rather than arguing for the intrinsic value of writing courses to advance humanities education, nurture the spiritual growth of the students, produce quality cultural workers, or any combinations of these—as has happened in most peer institutions and programs—Yan's vision for a university-based creative writing program most closely resembles the studio model that the IWW embodies. In other words, he emphasizes how academic courses enhance the cultivation of a creative writer rather than how writing courses supplement general academic training. For him, creative writing remains front and center at RUC's creative writing program, though his teaching experience at HKUST reverts to the other model of integrating creative writing into the humanistic curriculum.

Regardless of whether serendipitous leadership support and "celebrity" endorsement can yield consistent and sustainable results in developing writing programs for the long run, the examples above have made for exhilarating founding narratives, a nontrivial feat in writing faculties' efforts of program building in China. Yet the story gets trickier when it is seen from the other end of the equation: student learning experiences. The defenders of Chinese writing programs assert that students can apply what they have learned in writing classes to different lines of work and other areas of life after graduation. The acquisition of "common sense, taste, and appreciation of literature and the humanities," along with specific writing and communication skills, rank among the most common items mentioned as returns for the time and resources individual students and their families have invested in writing programs. Of course, the high employment rate of their graduates, and the prestigious degrees and awards they have won later, would never go amiss. Does the value of creative writing programs consist solely in an increase in students' marketability, however? Are Chinese students' goals different from those of their American counterparts, who, according to some, swarm to writing programs mainly for "the experience"?[23] Does the apparent enhancement of their employment prospects, though no small thing while being faced with the prevailing trends of "the decline of the humanities" and increasingly fierce competition among college graduates in a pandemic-ravaged economy, reveal the devaluation and even demise of the true spirit of providing a humanistic education and educating well-rounded individuals? How much does the current state of the field owe to the specific Chinese sociopolitical context, and how much can we attribute it to the intrinsic precarity of creative writing programs in a science-oriented university setting, something that is also true in the United States?[24] Even though it is perhaps impossible to produce definitive answers, it would be worthwhile to examine anew the circuit of cultural production in which individuals, programs, institutions, and governments interact with and counteract each other in postsocialist China at an even more precarious postpandemic moment.

5

EPILOGUE

WE WILL NOT BE REPLACED
BY CHATGPT?

"ChatGPT would not pose a threat to us."[1] Thus stated Wang Anyi and Yu Hua with apparent confidence at a forum held at ECNU on March 26, 2023. Hosted by Huang Ping at ECNU's Research Institute of Chinese Creative Writing (see chapter 3), this event provided the two esteemed guests—as well as the faculty and students of the host institution—the opportunity to exchange ideas on various critical issues in Chinese literary production, such as the relationship between the avant-garde and realism in contemporary Chinese literature, the role of Chinese writers, and the rise of generative AI and its effect on creative writing. The two writers seemed to regard the 1980s and 1990s as not only a literary boom period of cultural ferment in China but also the forever-gone golden years for Chinese writers who, according to them, viewed literary creation as their sole mission in life at the time. Colored by nostalgia, their reminiscences carry even more poignancy given the Chinese people's recent struggles with the COVID-19 pandemic. After China's draconian handling of the pandemic for the majority of three years, the party-state made a sudden about-face in December 2022, ending their zero-COVID policy abruptly without prior warning to the public or adequate preparation. Within two weeks, it led to tens of thousands of COVID-related deaths and untold economic and social damage in China.

Since November 2009, when the first MFA in creative writing was launched at Fudan University with Wang Anyi at its helm, Chinese creative writing programs have grown exponentially. Yet an avalanche of societal changes in China, including but not limited to those created by a three-year global pandemic and the recent release of ChatGPT 4.0, has given rise to many thorny issues. While more and more Chinese institutions have established creative writing programs and have offered related courses, producing crops of students year by year who earn degrees in creative writing, recent graduates have found that their job prospects have worsened precipitously as the Chinese economy has struggled to break free from the choke hold of the state's zero-COVID policy and its aftermath. Those fortunate enough to have landed well-paying jobs, such as in civil service or the corporate world, moreover, have expressed disillusionment and discontent either with the suffocating bureaucratic system or the rat race of business and commerce.[2]

It is not just individual alumni but also the writing programs that are wrestling with irresolvable tensions. Prestigious institutions have continued to invest in building up writing programs. Most recently, nine high-ranked universities, including PKU, BNU, RU, Qinghua, Fudan, NJU, ECNU, Tongji, and Shanghai Jiaotong University (SJTU), formed the "League of University-Based Creative Writing Programs," seemingly heralding a postpandemic recovery and period of growth for creative writing in China.[3] However, programmatic expansion sets up a sharp contrast with increasing constrictions on the freedom of speech. Following the recent success of Sun Ganlu's *One Thousand Miles of Rivers and Mountains* (see chapter 3), which was hailed by mainstream media and cultural institutions as a "new red classic," Ge Hongbing, another contemporary author and the director of the creative writing program at SHU (see chapter 1), led a creative writing workshop at the Resistance Museum of Sihang 四行Warehouse, a historical site that had witnessed the Nationalist Army's resistance against the Japanese invasion of Shanghai in 1937. He encouraged the participants to discover creative ideas from historical sources and write "good resistance stories" that could "expose the ugly face of Japanese fascists" and rally the reader against the "hegemonic discursive power of the West."[4] Previously known for spearheading SHU's creative writing program, which emphasizes its training of writers of popular as well as serious literature, Ge has answered Xi Jinping's call to "tell Chinese stories better," demonstrating yet again the Chinese writers' and creative writing programs' necessarily acrobatic maneuvers in response to state ideologies. Furthermore, the CCP reach has expanded and taken a firmer hold in Hong Kong in recent years, sending repercussions across their cultural ecosystem as well. Additionally, the escalating tension between mainland China and Taiwan, aided and abetted by the US government, is impeding academic and cultural exchanges across the Taiwan Strait, as I found out at my expense when I failed to secure a visitor's visa from Taiwan's immigration authorities in summer 2023.

Politics has always played an oversized role in literary production in the PRC, which has been demonstrated once again by recent developments. At times, it can work as a generative as well as disciplinary force in literary production. As mentioned, the flourishing of the Chinese avant-garde movement in the 1980s can be attributed to state sponsorship, which allowed Ma Yuan, Li Tuo 李陀, Ge Fei, and many other emerging writers to publish their artistic experiments in leading mainstream literary journals while garnering commercial and reputational gains (chapter 3). More recently, former avant-garde Chinese writers such as Sun Ganlu and Yu Hua have also shifted their writing styles and narrative modes to stay relevant and impactful under new political and market realities, and they have been amply rewarded by state-sponsored literary awards (see chapter 3). Thus, it would be unwise to dismiss ideologically informed and inflected literature as uncreative and to seek innovation only in works purportedly pursuing an autonomous aesthetic, even if that were at all possible in the Chinese context. Ideology, though often disparaged by Western scholars when judging literature, has always formed an integral component of cultural life in China rather than merely being a source of contamination.

Likewise, the apparently symbiotic relationship between Chinese writers and the party-state need not detract from the cultural entrepreneurship demonstrated in their endeavors to build creative writing curricula and programs in China. As has been shown, the thriving of university-based creative writing programs in China over the last fifteen years has depended on faculty members and administrators first making a successful pitch to the higher-ups and then taking advantage of official cultural policies and educational initiatives as well as state financial support (see chapter 4). In fact, in the short history of Chinese writing programs, one can detect themes parallel to those of their American models' founding narratives. Paul Engle was, in the words of writer Kurt Vonnegut, "a glamorous planetary citizen on the order of Duke Ellington or Charlie Chaplin."[5] Known for his marketing and fundraising prowess, which was essential to the expansion of the IWW and the establishment of the IWP (see chapter 1), he also wielded the IWP as a tool of soft diplomacy for the US government during and after the Cold War (see chapter 2). Today, the IWP still receives funding from the US State Department for its various cultural programming across the globe, including in China. Similarly, the successful launch and continual growth of creative writing programs in China would not have come to fruition without the trailblazing efforts of Chinese writers and scholars to secure state aid.

The professionalization of creative writing has apparently taken a different path in the three East Asian sites I have looked at here than it has in the United States. Wang Anyi and her colleagues have not only successfully lobbied the Chinese Ministry of Education and senior leadership at their institutions, but they have also adapted the classic workshop-style of teaching creative writing to suit local circumstances and needs: classes with higher enrollments, more introverted and reserved students, and more top-down state controls compared to their American peers' experiences. Moreover, writing faculty and administrators in mainland China, Hong Kong, and Taiwan have promoted the contributions of their curricular offerings to liberal arts education, national cultural construction, or the general well-being of students in academic, mental, and pragmatic terms, including their job prospects. In comparison, the US model, represented by the IWW, is seemingly less shackled by pragmatic concerns, emphasizing instead the faculty's expertise and their ability to offer specialized training in writing in different genres.

Yet the contrast between an academic and studio model, or between the divergent foci of academics and craft, may not be as stark as it has first appeared. Humanistic fields face similar challenges across the globe. The programmatic focus of Chinese writing programs may well trend toward enhanced apprenticeship as they gain stronger purchase in Chinese academic circles and push for more training to enhance their students' job prospects, while their US peers must also defend their curricula to anxious parents and the public. Most importantly, the promotion of creativity through pedagogy and cultural production, whatever the specific underlying motive may be, echoes the spirit if not the precise form of the American model and can open previously closed-off spaces for individual explorations in China.

Of the writing programs located at the three East Asian sites I have focused on in this book, mainland Chinese writing programs—apparently more so than their counterparts in Hong Kong and Taiwan—take pride in their espousal of a global perspective, as they seek to provide not only training grounds for domestic cultural workers but also venues for students to engage with world literature. Reflecting both state imperatives and Chinese intellectuals' individual priorities, this self-conscious pursuit may well have stemmed from a sense of anxiety and insecurity, as writers and scholars in mainland China combat stringent political controls and rising market pressures at home on the one hand, and perceived hostility or at least indifference to their works from abroad on the other. In some cases, it also dovetails with the writers' recent attempts to "tell good Chinese stories" to the outside world, seen by some as an effective strategy to gain global acceptance and accolades beyond the borders of mainland China. This latest development arguably provides yet another example of state power in Chinese cultural and literary production and Chinese intellectuals' strategic maneuvers under an authoritarian regime. But what calls for a deeper probing lies not so much in whether contemporary Chinese literature can or cannot measure up to the best of world literature based on the writers' proximity to state power or their works' level of political consciousness, as it does in why certain criteria of literary excellence have been embraced by Chinese writers as well as those from other nations in the first place.

Concepts of good taste, appropriate conduct, or aesthetic merit are not natural or universal; rather, they are rooted in social experience, and they reflect class interests. Rather than unquestioningly applying criteria such as an autonomous aesthetic to judge the quality of literary works, I posit that we use Chinese writer-instructors' diverse positions on how their national literature can "step into the world" to reexamine several recurring themes of modern Chinese cultural history: the role of literature in society, the identity of Chinese intellectuals, and Chinese people's changing structure of feelings. Chinese writers' and scholars' acceptance, modification, or contestation of Eurocentric criteria of world-class literature—ranging from "show, don't tell," the classic definition disseminated by American creative writing programs, to "the literature of the denial of life," which is endorsed by influential Western cultural institutions, including the Nobel Prize in Literature—can ultimately be traced to their struggles with perceived global cultural hierarchy and with their individual and collective identities.

As producers and consumers of Chinese literature tackle specific issues intrinsic to Chinese modernity, the spectrum of the writers' positions on the relationship between Chinese and world literatures speaks volumes not only of the continual evolution of contemporary Chinese literature under shifting market and political conditions but also of their individual resourcefulness and resiliency. Their work as writing instructors, administrators, and faculty members introduces generations of students to the often messy yet exciting realm of cultural production despite, or precisely because of, the restrictions and perimeters set by external forces beyond their control, whether these come from abroad or at home. Arif Dirlik has invented the term "postsocialism" to describe "a loss of faith in [socialism] as a social and political metatheory with a coherent present and a certain future."[6] The postsocialist condition is nowhere more recognizable than in the realm of literary and cultural production in contemporary China. Herein emerged a mixed space where the socialist publishing system lingers through regulation systems and continuing censorship, but commercialism also runs rampant, especially through web publishing and internet literature. There is still room for individual expression and creativity even in postsocialist Chinese cultural spaces, including at university-based creative writing programs, where new forms of communication and interaction are simultaneously integrated and contending with state-sponsored artistic and political ideals every day.

Mark McGurl pleads plaintively that we seek "the utopian element" in the American-style creative writing program, because "far from a noxious construction [it] is simply a complex and compromised one." He acknowledges that as a product of the Cold War and "part of the PR apparatus of liberal capitalism," creative writing in the United States—and the West in general—cannot escape those compromising bounds. Yet he also validates its core aspirations to help us "to be creative together," since "education should be responsive to our deepest desires for self-development and collective self-understanding."[7] In the same vein, despite the perhaps compromising connections of Chinese creative writing programs to the party-state, creative writing should be viewed as an intrinsic benefit. "It is something good, like knowledge, like ice cream," argues McGurl. When Wang Anyi and Yu Hua touted individual idiosyncrasies and imperfections in literary creation as a weapon against "the perfect and perfectly banal" fares produced by AI—utilizing its capability to scour, summarize, and "plagiarize" from vast data—they might have predicted the power of individualism and its appeal to contemporary audiences in an overly optimistic tone.[8] Yet in resisting ChatGPT, they have also recognized the illogic and irrationality of life and the diversity of human experiences and thereby affirmed humanistic values as an antidote to industrialized global capitalism. To say the least, creative writing gestures toward an alternative vision of success and fulfillment through creative endeavors, a rare commodity that can potentially help teachers and students alike to contend with and heal from wounds inflicted by the unrelenting neoliberal economic regulations and prescriptive cultural policies of postsocialist China.

NOTES

Chapter 1

[1] Karlinsky, editor, *Dear Bunny*, 300.

[2] McGurl, *The Program Era*, 4.

[3] Glass, *After the Program Era,* 5.

[4] Bennett, *Workshops of Empire,* 93.

[5] So, "The Invention of the Global MFA," 506.

[6] Author interview with James Shea, October 9, 2022.

[7] Mizumura, *The Fall of Language,* 40–41.

[8] Unpublished manuscript, "Beida Wenxue Jiangxi Suo Ti'an."

[9] Unpublished manuscript, "Fudan MFA Self-Study."

[10] Ibid.

[11] ECNU is envisioning curricular changes to focus more on the writing craft rather than knowledge of literary history and theories. Author's interview, November 2023.

[12] Simon, "Why Writers Love."

[13] Author interview with Chen Sihe, September 23, 2019.

[14] Author interview with Mu Ye, November 30, 2019.

[15] Gao, "An Overview," 1–3.

[16] Wang Pu, "Dui woguo wushi niandai," 8.

[17] Gao, "An Overview," 10–12.

[18] Author's interview with Shao Yanjun, April 27, 2023.

[19] See Wuhua Daxue.

[20] Wilbers, *The Iowa Writers' Workshop*, 61.

[21] Ibid., 62.

[22] Ibid., 71–72.

[23] Ibid., 88.

[24] Ibid., 83.

[25] McGurl, *The Program Era*, 363.

[26] Ibid., 23.

[27] Wilbers, 88.

[28] The Chinese Literature Department, "Self-Study."

Chapter 2

[1] E.g., see So, "The Invention of the Global MFA," 500.

[2] Wilbers, *Iowa Writers' Workshop*, 120.

[3] Liu, "Engagement, Reunion, Division," 620.

[4] Ibid., 612.

[5] Mizumura, *The Fall of Language*, 40–41.

[6] Engle, "Introduction," xvii.

[7] Bennett, *Workshops of Empire*, 115.

[8] Engle, "Introduction," xxv.

[9] "The New Colossus," accessed October 21, 2016, https://en.wikipedia.org/wiki/The_New_Colossus.

[10] Liu, "The World Comes to Iowa," 617.

[11] Bennett, 115.

[12] Ibid.

[13] Ibid.

[14] Engle, "Introduction," xxviii.

[15] Author's interview with Christopher Merrill, IWP director, summer 2017.

[16] Thomsen, *Mapping World Literature*, 103–138.

[17] Wang and Zhang, "Tanhua lu (er)," 30–48.

[18] The IWP staffers complain about their "catch-22" dilemma even today, for US immigration laws require English proficiency of all J-1 visitors, and they potentially exclude prominent writers whose language skills disqualify them (personal correspondence with Natasa Durovicova, December 18, 2016).

[19] Xia, "Xianzai de zuojia."

[20] Author's interview with Hua-Ling Engle, July 2016.

[21] Engle, "Introduction," xxvii.

[22] Riggan, "A Personal Encounter," 376.

[23] Torrevillas, "Blue Route to the Pentacrest," 378–381.

[24] Nazareth, "Adventures in International Writing," 382–387.

[25] Ivask, "Introduction," 365.

[26] Nieh and Engle, *The Poetry of Mao Tse-Tung*, 21.

[27] Ibid.

[28] Liu, "The World Comes to Iowa," 621.

[29] Miggang, "Chinese Weekend in Iowa."

[30] Engle, "Introduction," xxvii.

[31] Paul Engle and Hua-ling Nieh were married in 1971, at which point she adopted Engle as her legal surname. To avoid confusion, in this chapter, I will cite their full names.

[32] Liu, "The World Comes to Iowa," 612.

[33] Shea, "Co-opting the International Writing Program," 79.

[34] Wure Ertu, "Images of America," Black Binders Series, Box 5 (1983–1988), IWPR.

[35] Ding, "The Football Game," 178. This essay found its way into *The World Comes to Iowa*, and some lines were quoted as an epigraph by Peter Zhou (1993: 5–16), UI East Asian librarian, for a search guide that prefaces a special collection featuring all the IWP's Chinese alumni.

[36] Ibid., 177.

[37] Xiao, "Revelations in Iowa," 164.

[38] Xiao, "Some Judgments about America," 183–192.

[39] Xiao and Kinkley, *Traveller Without a Map*, 265.

[40] Xia, "Xianzai de zuoja."

[41] Engle letter, Xiao Qian folder, International Writing Program Records (IWPR), Special Collections, UI.

[42] Xiao, "Some Judgments about America," 191.

[43] Wang Meng, "Farewell, Iowa," 235.

[44] Wang and Zhang.

[45] Wang, "Ba" (Postscript), *Munü tongyou Meilijian*, 400.

[46] Wure Ertu, "Images of America," Black Binders Series, Box 5 (1983–1988), IWPR.

[47] Ru and Wang, 204.

[48] Ibid., 290.

[49] Mizumura, 30.

[50] Ru and Wang, 185.

[51] Ibid., 194.

[52] Wang and Zhang, 39.

[53] Ibid.

[54] Wang, "Ba," 398.

[55] Ru and Wang, 142.

[56] Ibid., 196.

[57] Ibid., 169.

58 Ibid., 196.

59 Ibid., 160.

60 Ibid., 244.

61 Deng and Ge, "Duihua Ge Fei," 26.

62 Ru and Wang, 69.

63 Ibid., 8, 13, 23.

64 Ibid., 269.

65 Ibid., 152.

66 Ibid., 240.

67 Ibid., 288.

68 Ibid., 174.

69 Ibid., 216.

70 Nieh, *Sansheng sanshi*, 340.

71 Ru and Wang, 317.

72 Ibid., 90.

73 Chen, "Wang Anyi, Taiwan, and the World."

74 Wang and Zhang, 39.

75 "Yingtenaxiongnaier," accessed February 27, 2023, https://view.inews.qq.com/k/20211122A02DLO00?web_channel=wap&openApp=false&pgv_ref=baidutw.

76 "Wutuobang shipian," accessed February 27, 2023, https://www.douban.com/group/topic/91431413/?_i=7532712AtDIlRK.

77 It is now known as the famous Lu Xun School of Literature (Lu Xun Wenxue Yuan). See Wang Anyi, "Huiyi Wenxue Jiangxi Suo," http://www.chinawriter.com.cn/bk/2010-12-22/49505.html.

78 Rojas, "Mothers and Daughters," 35–42.

79 Wang and Zhang, 40.

80 Wang and Zhang, 38.

81 Huang, "Ru Zhijuan, Chen Yingzhen," 26.

82 Chen, "Wang Anyi, Taiwan, and the World," 54.

83 Wang, "Cong he er lai," 304.

84 Chen, "Wang Anyi, Taiwan, and the World," 52.

85 "Yingtenaxiongnaier."

86 Ibid.

87 Wang and Zhang, 40.

88 "2019 Shanghai Xiezuo Jihua," 4.

[89] Ru and Wang, 143.

[90] Ibid., 160.

[91] Bi and Deng, "Bi Feiyu," 87, 90.

[92] Deng and Ge, 26.

[93] Mizumura, 40.

[94] Ge Haowen [Howard Goldblatt], "Zhongguo wenxue ruhe zou chuqu?"

[95] Deng, "Zhongguo dangdai wenxue."

[96] Damrosch, *What Is World Literature?* 281.

[97] Zhang, "Mapping Chinese Literature," 6.

[98] Shih, "Global Literature and the Technologies of Recognition."

[99] Apter, *Against World Literature.*

[100] Zhang, "Mapping Chinese Literature," 6.

[101] Chen Rong folder, IWPR.

[102] Can Xue folder, IWPR.

[103] Deng and Ge, 27.

[104] Ibid.

Chapter 3

[1] Xi Jinping, "Report on the Twentieth National Party Congress," https://www.12371.cn/2022/10/25/ARTI1666705047474465.shtml, accessed March 4, 2023.

[2] English translation of Xi Jinping's report, https://www.feiqiaoshang.com/portal/article/index/id/20463/navigation/0.html, accessed March 4, 2023.

[3] Renmin Wang, "Jianghao Zhongguo gushi," https://baijiahao.baidu.com/s?id=1735846307097715158&wfr=spider&for=pc, accessed March 1, 2023.

[4] The May Fourth New Culture Movement (1919–1937), named after the student demonstration against foreign encroachment that happened on May 4, 1919, is generally held as the first collective Chinese native movement toward modernization that led to pervasive cultural and sociopolitical transformations. For more details, see Goldman, "Introduction."

[5] This concept was first used by Raymond Williams in his *A Preface to Film* (with Michael Orrom, 1954), developed in *The Long Revolution* (1961) and elaborated throughout his work, in particular *Marxism and Literature* (1977). Williams used it to characterize the lived experience or the quality of life at a particular time and place. See Taylor, "Structure of Feelings."

[6] Prasad, "Ideology of the Hindi Film," 103.

[7] Lin, "Radical Iconoclasm," 6.

[8] Metzger, *Escape from Predicament*, 134.

[9] Mao Zedong, "Talks at the Yan'an Forum."

[10] Hong, *Zhongguo dangdai wenxue shi*, 259.

[11] Barboza, "China Surpasses US."

[12] Linder, "Web Literature," 896.

[13] Hills, *Fan Cultures*, 180.

[14] Hall, "Notes on Deconstructing," 228.

[15] Author's interview, September 2019.

[16] Author's interview, April 27, 2023.

[17] This series was published by the Institute of the Teaching and Learning of Literature at PKU on WeChat from September 1 to October 18, 2021, under the special topic, "How Is the Author Made?"

[18] Huang Ping, "Xiaoshuo de jingzheng," https://3g.k.sohu.com/t/n665561045, accessed March 3, 2023.

[19] See Xu Yang, "Sun Ganlu."

[20] Sun, *Qianli jiangshan*, 51.

[21] Ibid., 182.

[22] Ibid., 87.

[23] Ibid., 45.

[24] Ibid., 23.

[25] Ibid., 316, 356.

[26] Ibid., 305.

[27] Fu, "Zuihou de xianfeng."

[28] Dirlik, "Postsocialism?" 374.

[29] Zhang, *Postsocialism and Cultural Politics*, 10.

[30] Wang, "Zai pingyong de shisu li."

[31] Han Han, "Wang Anyi xinzuo."

[32] Deng Anqing, "Yi ba dao, qiange zi."

[33] Wang, *Yi ba dao*, 10.

[34] Ibid., 298.

[35] Ibid., 111.

[36] Ibid., 11.

[37] Ibid., 112.

[38] Ibid., 24–25.

[39] Ibid., 241.

[40] Ibid., 189.

[41] Ibid., 11.

[42] Ibid., 295.

[43] Wang, "Zai pingyong de shisu li."

[44] Lee, *Revolution of the Heart*, 301.

[45] Berlant, *Cruel Optimism*, 95–96.

[46] Fu, "Zuihou de xianfeng."

[47] Can Xue, "Zhongguo dangdai zuojia de zibei qingjie," http://www.360doc.com/content/19/1011/20/32528921_866208257.shtml, accessed March 3, 2023.

[48] Hockx, *Internet Literature*, 27.

[49] Barmés, *In the Red,* 311.

Chapter 4

[1] McGurl, *The Program Era*, 4.

[2] The IWP played a crucial role in the development of Hong Kong's first Chinese-language creative writing course (called Poetry Writing Workshop), and it fostered a poetics that continues to flourish in Hong Kong today. See Shea, "From Iowa City."

[3] Hua-ling Nieh Engle recalls being the first fiction writing teacher in Taiwan: "In 1962, Mr Tai [Ching-lung] invited me in person to teach fiction writing at the Department of Chinese, National Taiwan University, where he was the Chair. It was the first program of its kind in Taiwan." See Nieh, *San beizi*, 237.

[4] Author's interview with Shao Yanjun, April 27, 2023.

[5] Author's interview with Cao Wenxuan, November 5, 2019.

[6] Author's interview with Diao Keli, November 4, 2019.

[7] Author's interview with Wang Anyi, September 29, 2019.

[8] Author's interview with Chu Yunxia, November 8, 2019.

[9] Simon, "Why Writers Love to Hate the M.F.A."

[10] The above discussion is excerpted from Abramson, "From Modernism to Metamodernism."

[11] Author's interview, September 2019.

[12] Author's interview, January 2023.

[13] Author's interview with Zhang Yiwei, September 18, 2019.

[14] Author's interview with Yan Dong, September 17, 2019.

[15] Author's interview with Dong Yue, September 19, 2019.

[16] Shea, "Radical Translation."

[17] Author's interview with James Shea, October 9, 2022.

[18] Shea, "Three Case Studies," 8.

[19] Author's interviews with Tang Yui, January 16 and 17, 2023.

[20] Author's interview with Luo Leming, a Hong Kong-based writer and editor of *Zihua* (Fleur de Lettres), January 16, 2023.

[21] Author's interview, December 2019.

[22] Siegel, "Teaching Creative Writing," 158.

[23] McGurl, *The Program Era*, 14.

[24] Ibid., 363.

Chapter 5

[1] Yuan Huan, "Wang Anyi, Yu Hua duitan," http://www.chinawriter.com.cn/n1/2023/0327/c403994-32651769.html, accessed April 22, 2023.

[2] Author's interviews, January through April 2023.

[3] *Beijing qingnian bao*, "Jiusuo gaoxiao," https://www.chinanews.com.cn/cul/2023/04-09/9986585.shtml, accessed April 22, 2023.

[4] Zhao Tianhu, "Zuojia Ge Hongbing," https://cyxz.shu.edu.cn/info/1024/2073.htm, accessed April 22, 2023.

[5] J. Carlson, "Late Leader Engle."

[6] Dirlik, "Postsocialism?" 374.

[7] McGurl, "Afterword," 254.

[8] Yuan Huan, "Wang Anyi, Yu Hua duitan."

Appendix

Catalog of Interviews

Interviewee names are listed in chronological order for each time period listed below.

I. September–October 2019, Shanghai: Tao Lei 陶磊 (Fudan), Zhang Yiwei 张怡微 (Fudan), Zhang Yanbing 张岩冰 (Fudan), Wang Hongtu 王宏图 (Fudan), Zhang Sheng 张生 (Tongji), Yan Dong 阎冬 (Fudan), Huang Xinping 黄馨平 (Fudan), Dong Yue 董玥 (Fudan), Ge Hongbing 葛红兵 (SHU), Chen Sihe 陈思和 (Fudan), Fu Yuehui 甫跃辉 (Fudan alum and editor), Wang Anyi 王安忆 (Fudan), Deng Rubing 邓如冰 (UIBE, virtual).

II. November 2019, Beijing: Diao Keli 刁克利 (RUC), Cao Wenxuan 曹文轩 (PKU), Weng Yanqing 翁彦卿 (PKU), Zhang Qinghua 张清华 (BNU), Chu Yunxia 褚云侠 (UIBE, virtual), Yang Qingxiang 杨庆祥 (RUC, virtual).

III. December 2019, Kaohsiung, Taiwan: Lü Qifen 吕奇芬 (NKNU).

IV. October 2020, Grinnell, Iowa, USA: Ralph Savarese (GC, virtual), Dean Bakopoulos (GC, virtual), Paula Smith (GC, virtual).

V. January 2021, Grinnell, Iowa, USA: Wen Guiliang 文贵良 (ECNU, virtual).

VI. September 2021, Grinnell, Iowa, USA: Peter Nazareth (UI, virtual).

VII. August–October 2022, Grinnell, Iowa, USA: Liu Jianmei 刘剑梅 (HKUST, virtual), Lo Shih-lung 罗仕龙 (NTHU, virtual), Yan Lianke 阎连科 (RUC and HKUST, virtual), Ge Liang 葛亮 (HKBU, virtual), James Shea (HKBU, virtual).

VIII. December 2022, China: Yan Dong (virtual), Dong Yue (virtual).

IX. January 2023, Hong Kong: Howard Choy (HKBU), James Shea (HKBU), Chris Tong (Tong Yui 唐睿, HKBU), Yu Long Kit 余龙杰 (HKBU), Luo Lemin 罗乐敏 (HK poet).

X. April 2023, Grinnell, Iowa, USA: Shao Yanjun (PKU, virtual).

XI. May 2023, Grinnell, Iowa, USA: Yang Chia-hsien 杨佳娴 (NTHU, virtual).

XII. August 2023, Nanjing, China: Bi Feiyu 毕飞宇 (NJU).

XIII. September 2023, Beijing, China: Deng Rubing (UIBE), Chu Yunxia (UIBE), Shao Yanjun (PKU), Li Er 李洱 (PKU), Fan Yingchun 范迎春 (PKU), Cong Zhichen 丛治辰 (PKU).

XIV. November 2023, Shanghai, China: Wen Guiliang (ECNU), Sun Ganlu 孙甘露 (ECNU), Huang Ping 黄平 (ECNU), Li Xiaoqing 李晓晴 (ECNU), Fu Yuehui 甫跃辉 (ECNU), Wang Hongtu (Fudan), Wu Jun 吴俊 (SJTU).

BIBLIOGRAPHY

Abramson, Seth. "From Modernism to Metamodernism: Quantifying and Theorizing the Stages of the Program Era." In *After the Program Era: The Past, Present, and Future of Creative Writing in the University*, edited by Loren Glass, 233–248. Iowa City: University of Iowa Press, 2016.

Apter, Emily. *Against World Literature: On the Politics of Untranslatability*. London: Verso, 2013.

Aubry, Timothy. "'Workshops of Empire' by Eric Bennett," *New York Times*, November 25, 2015, www.nytimes.com/2015/11/29/books/review/workshops-of-empire-by-eric-bennett.html?_r=0.

Barboza, David. "China Surpasses U.S. in Number of Internet Users." *New York Times*, July 26, 2008.

Barmés, Geremie. *In the Red: On Contemporary Chinese Culture*. New York: Columbia University Press, 1999.

Bennett, Eric. *Workshops of Empire: Stegner, Engle, and American Creative Writing during the Cold War*. Iowa City: University of Iowa Press, 2015.

Bi Feiyu 毕飞宇 and Deng Rubing 邓如冰. "Bi Feiyu: Zhongguo wenxue yiran shi ruoshi de--guanyu Aihehua 'Guoji xiezuo jihua' yu 'dangdai Hanyu xiezuo guojihua' de duihua" 毕飞宇：中国文学依然是弱势的－关于爱荷华"国际写作计划"与"当代汉语写作国际化"的对话 (Bi Feiyu: Chinese Literature Is Still Disadvantaged—Dialogue on the International Writing Program in Iowa and the Internationalization of Contemporary Chinese Literature). *Xihu* 8 (2013): 87–90.

Can Xue 残雪. "Can Xue: Zhongguo dangdai zuojia de zibei qingjie" 残雪：中国当代作家的自卑情结 (Can Xue: The Inferiority Complex of Contemporary Chinese Writers), 2019, http://www.360doc.com/content/19/1011/20/32528921_866208257.shtml.

Carlson, J. "Late Leader Engle Kept Writers' Workshop in Full Shout," *Des Moines Register*, June 2, 1999.

Chen, Kuan-hsing. *Asia as Method: Toward Deimperialization*, Durham: Duke University Press, 2010.

Chen, Po-hsi. "Wang Anyi, Taiwan, and the World: The 1983 International Writing Program and Biblical Allusions in Utopian Verses." *Chinese Literature Today* 6, no.2 (2017): 52–61.

Christian, Barbara. "The Race for Theory." *Feminist Studies* 14, no. 1 (Spring 1988): 67–79.

Damrosch, David. *What Is World Literature?* Princeton: Princeton University Press, 2003.

Deng Anqing 邓安庆. "*Yi ba dao, Qiange zi*: Yanhuoqi li de geren shi" 《一把刀，千个字》：烟火气里的个人史 (The Knife and Words: Individual History in the Smell of Smoke and Fire). Zhongguo qingnian wang 中国青年网, May 25, 2021. https://baijiahao.baidu.com/s?id=17006781565346217 44&wfr=spider&for=pc.

Deng Changliang 邓长亮. "Zhongguo dangdai wenxue pingjia zhong de wenti, lichang yu fangfa: cong Hanxuejia Gu Bin yinfa de zhenglun tanqi" 中国当代文学评价中的问题，立场与方法：从汉学家顾彬引发的争论谈起 (Issues, Positions, and Methods in the Evaluation of Contemporary Chinese Literature: On the Controversy Caused by Sinologist Kubin). *Changchun ligong daxue xuebao (shehui kexue ban)* 24, no. 11 (November 2011): 80–81, 116.

Deng Rubing 邓如冰 and Ge Fei 格非. "Duihua Ge Fei: Zouxiang shijie de dangdai Hanyu xiezuo" 对话格非：走向世界的当代汉语写作 (Dialogue with Ge Fei: Contemporary Chinese Writings that Step into the World). *Jianghan daxue xuebao* 31, no. 6 (December 2012): 24–27.

Diao Keli 刁克力. *Zuozhe* 作者 (*The Author*). Beijing: Waiyu Jiaoxue Yu Yanjiu Chubanshe, 2019.

Ding Ling. "The Football Game," tr. Katherine Lu. In *The World Comes to Iowa*, edited by Paul Engle and Rowena Torrevillas, 176–178. Ames: Iowa State University Press, 1987.

Dirlik, Arif. "Postsocialism? Reflections on 'Socialist with Chinese Characteristics.'" In *Marxism and the Chinese Experience*, edited by Arif Dirlik and Maurice Meisner, 362–384. Armonk, NY: M. E. Sharpe, 1989.

Duara, Prasenjit. "Asia Redux: Conceptualizing a Region for Our Times." *Journal of Asian Studies* 69, no. 4 (2010): 963–983.

Dudley, Andrew. "An Atlas of World Cinema." In *Remapping World Cinema: Identity, Culture and Politics in Film*, edited by Stephanie Dennison and Song Hwee Lim, 19–29. London: Wallflower Press, 2006.

Engle, Paul. "Introduction." In *The World Comes to Iowa*, edited by Paul Engle and Rowena Torrevillas, xv–xxii. Ames: Iowa State University Press, 1987.

Fu Yicheng 傅逸尘. "Zuihou de xianfeng: Caixiang Sun Ganlu—cong *Huxi* dao *Qianli jiangshan tu*." 最后的先锋：猜想孙甘露——从《呼吸》到《千里江山图》 (The Last Avant-Garde: Guessing Sun Ganlu, from *Breathing* to *The Painting of One Thousand Miles of Rivers and Mountains*). *Zhongguo dangdai wenxue yanjiu* 中国当代文学研究, November 24, 2022, http://www.chinawriter.com.cn/n1/2022/1124/c404030-32573496.html.

Gao, Xiaojuan. "An Overview of the Development of Creative Writing Teaching and Research in Mainland China (2009–2020)." *New Writing* (2021): 1–38.

Ge Haowen 葛浩文 (Howard Goldblatt). "Zhongguo wenxue ruhe zou chuqu?" 中国文学如何走出去 (How Can Chinese Literature Step out?), *Wenxue bao*, July 7, 2014. http://history.sina.com.cn/cul/zl/2014-07-07/113094803.shtml.

Glass, Loren. "Introduction." In *After the Program Era: The Past, Present, and Future of Creative Writing in the University*, edited by Loren Glass, 1–8. Iowa City: University of Iowa Press, 2016.

Goldman, Merle. "Introduction." In *Modern Chinese Literature in the May Fourth Era*, edited by Merle Goldman, 1–14. Cambridge: Harvard University Press, 1977.

Gu Bin 顾彬 (Wolfgang Kubin). "Zhongguo dangdai wenxue shi laji" 中国当代文学是垃圾 (Contemporary Chinese Literature Is Trash), November 9, 2009, http://book.ifeng.com/culture/whrd/200911/1109_7467_1426359.shtml.

Hall, Stuart. "Notes on Deconstructing 'The Popular.'" In *People's History and Socialist Theory*, edited by Robert Samuel, 227–240. London and New York: Routledge, 1981.

Han Han 韩寒. "Wang Anyi xinzuo Yi badao, qiange zi: Mei dao xiaqu, doushi chengdiandian de rensheng" 王安忆新作《一把刀，千个字》：每刀下去，都是沉甸甸的人生 (Wang Anyi's New Work *The Knife and Words*: Every Slice Is Heavy Life). *Guangming ribao* kehuduan 光明日报客户端, May 10, 2021, https://baijiahao.baidu.com/s?id=1699362801231903519&wfr=spider&for=pc.

Hills, Matt. *Fan Cultures*. London and New York: Routledge, 2002.

Hockx, Michel. *Internet Literature in China*. New York: Columbia University Press, 2015.

Hong Zicheng 洪子诚. *Zhongguo dangdai wenxue shi* 中国当代文学史 (*History of Contemporary Chinese Literature*). Beijing: Beijing Daxue Chubanshe, 1999.

Hsia, C. T. *A History of Modern Chinese Fiction*. New Haven: Yale University Press, 1971.

Hu Shi. "Some Modest Proposals for the Reform of Literature." In *Modern Chinese Literary Thought: Writings on Literature, 1893–1945*, edited by Kirk Denton, 125–139. Stanford: Stanford University Press, 1996 [1917].

Huang Ping 黄平. "Xiaoshuo de jingzheng: *Songjiang yiwen lu* chuangzuo tan" 小说的竞争：《松江异闻录》创作谈 (The Competition of Fiction: On Writing *Strange Tales from Songjiang*), 2023, https://3g.k.sohu.com/t/n665561045.

Huang Wenqian 黄文倩. "Ru Zhijuan, Chen Yingzhen yu Wang Anyi de yuanyuan yu wenxue yingxiang kaocha" 茹志鹃，陈映真与王安忆的渊源与文学影响考察 (Interactions and Literary Influence between Ru Zhijuan, Chen Yingzhen, and Wang Anyi). *Wenyi zhengming*, no. 12 (2015): 14–24.

Ivask, Ivar. "Introduction." *World Literature Today* 61, no. 3 (Summer 1987): 365–367.

Jenkins, Henry. *Textual Poachers: Television Fans and Participatory Culture*. London and New York: Routledge, 1992.

Karlingsky, Simon, ed. *Dear Bunny, Dear Volodya: The Nabokov-Wilson Letters, 1940–1971*, revised and expanded edition. Berkeley: University of California Press, 2001.

Kong, Shuyu. *Consuming Literature: Best Sellers and the Commercialization of Literary Products in Contemporary China*. Stanford: Stanford University Press, 2005.

Lee, Haiyan. *Revolution of the Heart: A Genealogy of Love in China, 1900–1950*. Stanford: Stanford University Press, 2007.

Lee, Leo Ou-fan. *Shanghai Modern: The Flowering of a New Urban Culture in China 1930–1945*. Cambridge: Harvard University Press, 1999.

Lin, Yü-sheng. *The Crisis of Chinese Consciousness: Radical Anti-Traditionalism in the May Fourth Era*. Madison: University of Wisconsin Press, 1979.

Lin, Yü-sheng. "Radical Iconoclasm in the May Fourth Period and the Future of Chinese Liberalism." In *Reflections on the May Fourth Movement: Symposium*, edited by Benjamin Schwartz and Charlotte Furth. Cambridge: Harvard University Press, 1973.

Linder, Birgit. "Web Literature." In *Encyclopaedia of Contemporary Chinese Culture*, edited by Edward L. Davis, 647. London: Routledge, 2005.

Link, Perry. *Mandarin Ducks and Butterflies: Popular Fiction in Early Twentieth Century Chinese Cities*. Berkeley: University of California Press, 1981.

Liu Binyan. "Spacious Yet Confining." In *From the Outer World*, edited by Oscar Handlin and Lilian Handlin, 409–413. Cambridge: Harvard University Press, 1997.

Liu, Hongtao. "Chinese Literature's Route to World Literature," tr. David Z. Dayton. *CLCWeb: Comparative Literature and Culture*, Volume 17, no. 1 (2015), http://dx.doi.org/10.7771/1481-4374.2625.

Liu, Yi-hung. "The World Comes to Iowa in the Cold War: International Writing Program and the Translation of Mao Zedong." *American Quarterly* 69, no. 3 (September 2017): 611–631.

Liu, Yi-hung. "Engagement, Reunion, Division: 1979 Chinese Weekend in

Iowa City." *Inter-Asia Cultural Studies* 22, no. 1 (2021): 36–48.

Luo Haoling 罗皓菱. "Jiusuo gaoxiao lianhe chengli 'Zhonguo daxue chuangyi xiezuo lianmeng" 九所高校联合成立 "中国大学创意写作联盟" (Nine Institutions of Higher Education Formed 'University-Based Creative Writing League'"), *China News*, April 9, 2023, https://www.chinanews.com.cn/cul/2023/04-09/9986585.shtml.

Lyotard, Jean-François. *The Postmodern Condition: A Report on Knowledge*. Tr. Geoffrey Bennington and Brian Massumi. Minneapolis: University of Minnesota Press, 1984 [1979].

McGurl, Mark. "Afterword: And Then What?" In *After the Program Era: The Past, Present, and Future of Creative Writing in the University*, edited by Loren Glass, 249–255. Iowa City: University of Iowa Press, 2016.

McGurl, Mark. *The Program Era: Postwar Fiction and the Rise of Creative Writing*. Cambridge and London: Harvard University Press, 2009.

Mao Zedong. "Talks at the Yan'an Forum on Literature and Art," In *Modern Chinese Literary Thought, Part III, Revolutionary Literature 1923-1930*, edited by Kirk Denton, 458–484. Stanford: Stanford University Press, 1996 [1942].

Metzger, Thomas A. *Escape from Predicament: Neo-Confucianism and China's Evolving Political Culture*. New York: Columbia University Press, 1977.

Miggang, Herbert. "Chinese Weekend in Iowa," *New York Times*, August 17, 1979, https://iwp.uiowa.edu/sites/iwp/files/chineseweekend1979NYT.pdf.

Mizumura, Minae. *The Fall of Language in the Age of English.* Tr. Mari Yoshihara and Juliet Winters Carpenter. New York: Columbia University Press, 2015.

Muller, L. "Writing Program Spread the Word about U of I." *Gazette*, May 31, 1999.

Nazareth, Peter. "Adventures in International Writing." *World Literature Today* 61, no. 3 (Summer 1987): 382–387.

Nie Hualing 聂华苓. *Sansheng sanshi* 三生三世 (*Three Lives*). Tianjing: Baihua Wenyi Chubanshe, 2004.

Nie Hualing 聂华苓. *San Beizi* 三辈子 (*Three Lives*). Taipei: Linking Publishing, 2011.

Nieh, Hualing, ed. *Literature of the Hundred Flowers. Vol II: Poetry and Fiction.* New York: Columbia University Press, 1981.

Nieh, Hua-ling and Paul Engle, trans. *The Poetry of Mao Tse-Tung.* London: Wildwood House, 1973.

Prasad, M. Madhava. *Ideology of the Hindi Film: A Historical Construction.* Delhi: Oxford University Press, 1998.

Riggan, William. "A Personal Encounter with the International Writing Program: Notes and Thoughts." *World Literature Today* 61, no. 3 (Summer 1987): 375–378.

Rojas, Carlos. "Mothers and Daughters: Orphanage as Method." *Chinese Literature Today* 6, no. 2 (2017): 35–42.

Ru Zhijuan 茹志鹃 and Wang Anyi 王安忆. *Munü manyou Meilijian* 母女漫游美利坚 (*Mother and Daughter Toured the U.S.A.*). Shanghai: Shanghai Wenyi, 1986.

Ru Zhijuan 茹志鹃 and Wang Anyi 王安忆. *Munü tongyou Meilijian* 母女同游美利坚 (*Mother and Daughter Toured the U.S.A. Together*). Beijing: Zhongxin Chuban Jituan, 2018.

Shao Yanjun 邵燕君. *Xin shiji wenxue maixiang* 新世纪文学脉象 (*Pulse of Literature of the New Millennium*), Hefei: Anhui Jiaoyu Chubanshe, 2011.

Shea, James. "Co-Opting the International Writing Program during the Cold War: Gu Cangwu, the Baodiao Movement, and *Minjian* Activism." *Prism* 17, no. 1 (2020): 79–103.

Shea, James. "From Iowa City to Kowloon Tong: On the Cold War Origins of Creative Writing Pedagogy in Hong Kong." https://www.nawe.co.uk/DB/wip-editions/articles/from-iowa-city-to-kowloon-tong-on-the-cold-war-origins-of-creative-writing-pedagogy-in-hong-kong.html.

Shea, James. "Oulipo in Hong Kong: Welcoming Unconventional Forms in Poetry Writing Workshops." In *Poetry in Pedagogy,* edited by Dean A. F. Gui and Jason Polley, 27–43. New York: Routledge, 2021.

Shea, James. "Radical Translation: Teaching Poetry Writing in Hong Kong." In *Teaching Creative Writing in Asia*, edited by Darryl Whetter, 116–128. London and New York: Routledge, 2022.

Shea, James. "Teaching Chinese-Language Creative Writing in Hong Kong: Three Case Studies." *Text*, Special Issue 47: *Ideas and Realities: Creative Writing in Asia Today* (October 2017): 1–13.

Shih, Shu-mei. "Global Literature and the Technologies of Recognition." *PMLA: Publications of the Modern Language Association of America* 111, no. 1 (2004): 16–30.

Siegel, Robert Anthony. "Teaching Creative Writing in Taiwan, or, Taking the Worry out of the Word 'Creative.'" In *Teaching Creative Writing in Asia*, edited by Darryl Whetter, 157–162. London and New York: Routledge, 2022.

Simon, Cecilia Capuzzi. "Why Writers Love to Hate the M.F.A.," *New York Times*, April 9, 2015, https://www.nytimes.com/2015/04/12/education/edlife/12edl-12mfa.html.

So, Richard Jean. "Literary Information Warfare: Eileen Chang, the US State Department, and Cold War Media Aesthetics." *American Literature* 85, no. 4 (2013): 719–744.

So, Richard Jean. "The Invention of the Global MFA: Taiwanese Writers at Iowa, 1964–1980." *American Literary History* 29, no. 3 (2017): 499–520.

Sun Ganlu 孙甘露. *Qianli jangshan tu* 千里江山图 (*The Painting of One Thousand Miles of Rivers and Mountains*). Shanghai: Shanghai Wenyi, 2022.

Taylor, Jenny Bourne. "Structure of Feelings." In *A Dictionary of Cultural and Critical Theory*, edited by Michael Payne. London: Blackwell, 1997. http://www.blackwellreference.com/public/tocnode?id=g9780631207535_chunk_g978063120753522_ss1-37#citation._

Thomsen, Mads Rosendahl. *Mapping World Literature: International Canonization and Transnational Literatures*. London: Continuum, 2008.

Torrevillas, Rowena T. "Blue Route to the Pentacrest and a House on Bloomington Street." *World Literature Today* 61, no. 3 (Summer 1987): 378–381.

Wang Anyi 王安忆. "Cong he er lai, xiang he er qu" 从何而来，向何而去 (Came from Where and Will Go Where). In *Ta cong natiao lushang lai* 她从那条路上来 (*She Came that Way*), edited by Ru Zhijuan 茹志鹃, 304. Shanghai: Shanghai Wenyi, 2005.

Wang Anyi. "Ba" 跋 (Postscript). In Ru Zhijuan and Wang Anyi, *Munü tongyou Meilijian* 母女同游美利坚 (*Mother and Daughter Toured the U.S.A. Together*), 398–400. Beijing: Zhongxin Chuban Jituan, 2018.

Wang Anyi. *Xiaoshuo ketang* 小说课堂 (*Fiction Classroom*). Beijing: Renmin Wenxue Chubanshe, 2018.

Wang Anyi. *Yi ba dao, qiange zi* 一把刀，千个字 (*The Knife and Words*). Beijing: Renmin Wenxue Chubanshe, 2021.

Wang Anyi. "Zai pingyong de shisu li, du ziji de xiaohe" 在平庸的世俗里渡自己的小河 (Crossing One's Own Small River in the Mundane World), 2022, https://m.thepaper.cn/baijiahao_16198900.

Wang Anyi 王安忆 and Zhang Xinying 张新颖. "Tanhua lu (er): guanjiekou" 谈话录（二）：关节口 (Conversations (2): Key Moments). *Bohai daxue xuebao (zhexue shehui kexue ban)* no. 2 (March 2007): 30–48.

Wang Hui. *The Politics of Imagining Asia*, ed. Theodore Huters. Cambridge: Harvard University Press, 2011.

Wang Meng. "Farewell, Iowa." In *The World Comes to Iowa*, edited by Paul Engle and Rowena Torrevillas, 231–236. Ames: Iowa State University Press, 1987.

Wang Pu 王璞. "Dui woguo wushi niandai gaoxiao yuanxi tiaozheng deshi fenxi" 对我国 50 年代高校院系调整得失分析 (Analysis on Gains and Losses Caused by the Adjustment of Colleges and Departments in 1950s China). *Jiancai gaojiao lilun yu shijian* 20, no. 6 (December 2001): 7–10.

Wang Zengqi 汪曾祺. "Meiguo duan jian" 美国短简 (Short Notes on the U.S.). In Wang Zengqi 汪曾祺, *Tashang suibi* 塔上随笔 (*Jotted Notes in the Tower*), 58–68. Beijing: Qunzhong Chubanshe, 1993.

Whetter, Darryl, ed. *Teaching Creative Writing in Asia*. London and New York: Routledge, 2022.

Wilbers, Stephen. *The Iowa Writers' Workshop*. Iowa City: University of Iowa Press, 1980.

Wuhan Daxue Xiezuo Zazhishe 武汉大学《写作》杂志社. "Guanxuan le! Zhongwen chuangyi xiezuo chengwei Zhongguo yuyan wenxue xiashu erji xueke" 官宣了！中文创意写作成为中国语言文学下属二级学科 (Official announcement! Chinese Creative Writing has become a second-level discipline under Chinese Language and Literature). January 22, 2024. https://writing.whu.edu.cn/info/1019/1502.htm.

Xia Yu 夏榆. "Xianzai de zuojia meiyou qian yidai de shendu le: Nie Hualing zhuanfang" 现在的作家没有前一代的深度了：聂华苓专访 (Today's Authors Lack the Depth of Those Who Came Before: Interview of Nieh

Hualing). *Nanfang zhoumo*, July 24, 2008. http://www.infzm.com/content/15016.

Xiao Qian. "Revelations in Iowa." In *The World Comes to Iowa*, edited by Paul Engle and Rowena Torrevillas, 162–164. Ames: Iowa State University Press, 1987.

Xiao Qian. "Some Judgments about America." In *Land Without Ghosts: Chinese Impressions of America from the Mid-Nineteenth Century to the Present*, edited and translated by R. David Arkush and Leo O. Lee, 183–192. Berkeley: University of California Press, 1989.

Xiao Qian and Jeffrey C. Kinkley. *Traveller without a Map*. Stanford: Stanford University Press, 1993.

Xu Yang 许旸. "Sun Ganlu tan *Qianli jiangshan tu*: Wo chongxin chengwei 'chuxue zhe'" 孙甘露谈《千里江山图》：我重新成为 "初学者" (Sun Ganlu on *The Painting of One Thousand Miles of Rivers and Mountains*: I Will Become a New Learner Again). *Wenhui bao* 文汇报, December 21, 2022, https://m.yunnan.cn/system/2022/12/21/032395331.shtml.

Yang, Guobing. *The Power of the Internet in China: Citizen Activism Online*. New York: Columbia University Press, 2009.

Yangshi guoji 央视国际. "Deguo hanxuejia piping Zhongguo dangdai wenxue, xuezhe cheng qi wang xia jielun" 德国汉学家批评中国当代文学，学者称其妄下结论 (German Sinologist Criticized Contemporary Chinese Literature, and Chinese Scholars Called him 'Making Wrong Conclusions'), December 14, 2006. http://news.cctv.com/world/20061214/100494.shtml.

Yuan Huan 袁欢. "Wang Anyi, Yu Hua duitan: Rengong zhineng buhui mingbai, weida de wenxue zuopin doushi you baibi de" 王安忆余华对谈：AI 不会明白，伟大的文学作品都是有败笔的 (Dialogue between Wang Anyi and Yu Hua: AIs Won't Understand That All Great Literary Works Have Imperfections," March 27, 2023, http://www.chinawriter.com.cn/n1/2023/0327/c403994-32651769.html.

Zhang, Xudong. *Postsocialism and Cultural Politics: China in the Last Decade of the Twentieth Century*. Durham: Duke University Press, 2008.

Zhang, Yingjin. "Mapping Chinese Literature as World Literature." *CLCWeb: Comparative Literature and Culture*, Volume 17, no. 1 (2015), http://docs.lib.purdue.edu/clcweb/vol17/iss1/2.

Zhao Tianhu 赵天琥. "Zuojia Ge Hongbing deng juban 'Jubi wei qi, bu wang guochi' zhuti chuangyi xiezuo gongzuofang huodong" 作家葛红兵等举办 "举笔为旗，不忘国耻" 主题创意写作工作坊活动 (Author Ge Hongbing and Colleagues Held a Creative Writing Workshop Titled 'Raise our Pen as

Flag and Never Forget our Nation's Humiliations"), April 17, 2023, https://cyxz.shu.edu.cn/info/1024/2073.htm.

Zhou, Peter. 1993. "Chinese Writers in Iowa," *Books at Iowa 58*: 5-16. http://digital.lib.uiowa.edu/bai/zhou.htm.

Printed in the USA
CPSIA information can be obtained
at www.ICGtesting.com
JSHW020240080524
62711JS00002B/16